STUDENTS OF THE THIRD AGE

STUDENTS OF THE THIRD AGE

Richard B. Fischer, Senior Editor

Mark L. Blazey

Henry T. Lipman

nucea

National University Continuing Education Association
American Council on Education ▶◀ Macmillan Publishing Company
NEW YORK
Maxwell Macmillan Canada
TORONTO
Maxwell Macmillan International
NEW YORK   OXFORD   SINGAPORE   SYDNEY

Copyright © 1992 by American Council on Education and
    Macmillan Publishing Company,
    A Division of Macmillan, Inc.

All rights reserved. No part of this book may be reproduced or transmitted in any form or by any means, electronic or mechanical, including photocopying, recording, or by any information storage and retrieval system, without permission in writing from the Publisher.

Macmillan Publishing Company   Maxwell Macmillan Canada, Inc.
866 Third Avenue   1200 Eglinton Avenue East, Suite 200
New York, NY 10022   Don Mills, Ontario M3C 3N1

Macmillan Publishing Company is part of the
Maxwell Communication Group of Companies

Library of Congress Catalog Card Number: 91-26548

Printed in the United States of America

printing number
1 2 3 4 5 6 7 8 9 10

Library of Congress Cataloging-in-Publication Data

Students of the third age : university/college programs for retired
  adults / Richard B. Fischer (senior editor), Mark L. Blazey, Henry
  T. Lipman,
    p. cm.
  Includes bibliographical references and index.
  ISBN 0-02-897143-4
  1. Aged—Education (Higher)—United States. 2. Continuing
education—United States. 3. Universities and colleges—United
States. I. Fischer, Richard B. II. Blazey, Mark L. III Lipman.
Henry T.
LC5471.S78 1992   91-26548
                                                  CIP

The paper used in this publication meets the minimum requirements of American National Standard for Information Sciences—Permanence of Paper for Printed Library Materials. ANSI Z39.48-1984   ∞™

Contents

Acknowledgments ix

About the Authors xi

Introduction: Negotiating the Retirement Rite 1

Part I: THE NEW AGE WAVE AND HIGHER EDUCATION'S RESPONSE

1. **Post-Retirement Learning** 13
   Emerging Demographics and Social Patterns 14
   Higher Education Responses 18
   Issues and Questions 20
   Conclusion 21

Part II: DEVELOPING SUCCESSFUL COLLEGE-LEVEL PROGRAMS FOR LEARNING IN RETIREMENT

2. **LIR Program and Organization Models** 25
   Institution-Driven Programs 25
   Member-Driven Programs 26

	Common Characteristics	28
	Conclusion	36

3. Starting Your Own Learning-in-Retirement Program — 38

The Preconception Phase—Positioning for University Commitment	39
The Conception Phase—Keep the Message Simple	40
Gathering a Critical Mass of Community Support	41
The First Trappings of an Organization	41
Space—the First Frontier	42
The Program	43
Membership Dues	43
Political Support	44
Volunteer Structure	45
Role of Course Leaders/Peer Teachers	45
Initial Publicity	46
Converting Inquiries into Members	46
Quick Membership Growth	47
Governance Structure	48
Details Too Small to Mention	50
Conclusion	52

4. Instructional Program Design — 53

An Overview of LIR Programs	54
How the Curriculum Is Established	55
Formats and Levels of Participation	57
Selecting Instructional Leadership	59
Level of Academic Rigor	61
Maintaining Academic Standards	63
Auxiliary Educational Programs	65
Conclusion	66

5. Membership: Marketing, Recruitment, and Retention — 67

Marketing Thinking: What an Institute Offers Its Members	69
Attracting Members	72
Some Cautionary Notes About Marketing	77
Retention of Members: Thoughts on Member Satisfaction	78
Conclusion	82

6.	**Resource Allocation and Fee Setting**	84
	Institutional Issues	85
	Tuition and Membership Fee Structures	89
	Staff, Faculty, and Volunteers	92
	Developing and Managing the Budget	94
	Related Financial Issues	96
	Conclusion	98
7.	**The Intellectually Restless: Views from the Members**	99
	Psycho-Social Needs of Members	100
	Intellectual Benefits	103
	Social Benefits	104
	Maintaining a Sense of Purpose and Usefulness	106
	Controlling Your Life	107
	Health and Income Benefits	108

Part III: EXPANDED VISIONS AND NEW HORIZONS IN THE THIRD AGE

8.	**Intergenerational Synergy**	113
	Intergenerational Learning: A Working Definition	115
	Adult Development: Ages and Stages	116
	Intergenerational Learning: Program Characteristics and Institutional Applications	117
	Conclusion	120
9.	**Creative Retirement in an Aging Society**	122
	The Third-Age Learner in an Aging Society	122
	A Place for Creative Retirement	124
	Rationale for the Future	130
10.	**Coasting Home!**	132
	LIRs Belong to Their Members	134
	The Uses of the Past	138

APPENDIXES 141

I.	Learning-in-Retirement Bylaws	143
II.	Sample Membership Information Form	148
III.	Program Survey	150
IV.	Higher Education Institutions Sponsoring Member-Driven LIR-Type Programs	153
V.	Sample First-Year Annual LIR Budget	160
VI.	Memorandum of Understanding Concerning LIR Operations (Supplement to Bylaws)	162
VII.	Additional Resources	165

Bibliography 167

Index 171

Acknowledgments

We gratefully acknowledge the support and advice provided by Milton R. Stern, Dean Emeritus, University Extension, University of California—Berkeley; and Kay Kohl, Executive Director of the National University Continuing Education Association.

We also express thanks to Judy Crescenzi, Florence Garrett, Susan Holton, Barbara Singer, and Suzanne Smith, at the University of Delaware; and Peggy Murphy, of Johns Hopkins University, for their support and editorial eyes.

Finally, our special acknowledgment to Dr. Hyman Hirsch, who pioneered the first Institute for Retired Professionals at The New School for Social Research, and to the thousands of older adults who volunteer their time and talents to make learning-in-retirement programs work.

About the Authors

Mark L. Blazey, Ed.D., is Dean of Training and Professional Development for the Rochester Institute of Technology as well as Director of Training, Research and Services for the RIT Research Corporation. A former member of the Senior Executive Service in the federal government, with extensive top-level experience in the U.S. Department of Education, he was one of the founders, and served as first chairperson, of the National University Continuing Education Association's Division of Continuing Education for Older Adults. He also worked to create "The Athenaeum," Rochester's Academy for Older Adults at Rochester Institute of Technology, and helped to launch programs for older adults throughout the country. Dr. Blazey holds a doctorate in curriculum and instructional design and evaluation from the State University of New York at Albany.

James K. Broomall, Ed.D., is Associate Director, Program Development for the University of Delaware Division of Continuing Education. He received his Ed.D. in higher education (1984) from Pennsylvania State University. Dr. Broomall has held positions in educational leadership in both community college and university settings. His current responsibilities include oversight of the "Academy of Lifelong Learning" at the University of Delaware. His publications have appeared in the Jossey–Bass series *New Directions in Continuing Education, Community Services Catalyst, Journal of Adult Education,* and *Community College Review.*

Donald E. Collins is Associate Provost and Dean of the Division of Continuing Education and University College of Northwestern University. Before going to Northwestern, Mr. Collins served for many years in various decanal roles at New York University. It was his experience as neighbor to The New School for Social Research's "Institute for Retired Professionals" that led him to found the "Institute for Learning in Retirement" at Northwestern. He is a trustee of the Adler Planetarium in Chicago.

Sara Craven is Director of the Duke "Institute of Learning in Retirement," a part of the Duke University Office of Continuing Education. She has worked in counseling, teaching, and administrative positions with a wide variety of clients ranging from emotionally disturbed children to terminally ill patients and their families. Longstanding interest in both the humanities and older adults led her to the Duke Institute in 1987.

Jane S. Eesley is a former Assistant Director of Summer Session and Special Programs at Northwestern University. She has held positions in communications research, community development, and academic programming. A codeveloper of the "Institute for Learning in Retirement" at Northwestern, she also has spoken on LIR programs at conferences sponsored by the National University Continuing Education Association and the American Association of Retired Persons. Ms. Eesley currently works as a freelance writer.

Richard B. Fischer, Ed.D., is Associate Provost and Director, Division of Continuing Education, University of Delaware. He has an M.B.A. from Pennsylvania State University and a doctorate in adult and continuing education from Temple University. For the past twenty years he has been involved in the program development, marketing, and administration of one of the major continuing higher education programs in the United States. Dr. Fischer is a frequent presenter at national conferences, and has served as an officer of the National University Continuing Education Association.

Henry T. Lipman is Chairman of Elderhostel's Advisory Committee for University Institute programs, and a consultant on educational programs for older persons. A graduate of both Harvard College and American University, his professional work since 1938 has been devoted solely to the field of adult and continuing education. From 1957 to 1979 Mr. Lipman was at New York University, where he was professor of adult education and associate dean of the School of Continuing Education. For two years he was part of the NYU/USAID team in Nigeria, where he established and directed the continuing education program at the University of Lagos. After retiring from NYU in 1979, Mr. Lipman served until 1988 as Director of the "Institute for Retired Professionals" at The New School for Social Research in New York City.

Ronald J. Manheimer, Ph.D., is Executive Director of the North Carolina Center for Creative Retirement, and research professor of philosophy at the University of North Carolina–Asheville. He previously was Director of Older Adult Education for The National Council on Aging, Inc., Dr. Manheimer received his doctorate from the University of California–Santa Cruz, in the history of consciousness. He is the author of *Kierkegaard as Educator* (University of California Press, 1978) and other books and articles exploring philosophical aspects of human development.

About the Authors

Milton Stern was dean of university extension at the University of California–Berkeley, and is an honorary member of the University's "Center for Learning in Retirement." Before joining Berkeley in 1971, Mr. Stern was an associate professor in the graduate faculty of education at the University of Michigan, and also served as director of the University Center for Adult Education of the University of Michigan, Wayne State University, and Eastern Michigan University. Before that, he was director of liberal arts in extension at New York University. Mr. Stern is recognized nationally as one of the most gifted authors and lecturers in continuing higher education. His books include *Power and Conflict in Continuing Professional Education*, *The First Years in College*, and a marketing text entitled *People, Programs, and Persuasion*.

Kenneth E. Young, Ph.D., retired in 1989 as Director of the "Institute for Learning and Retirement" at American University, Washington, DC. He continues as senior associate with Eisenberg Associates, a Washington-based consulting firm. Dr. Young had a 42-year career in higher education, during which he served in faculty or administrative posts at six colleges and universities. He also was vice president of the American College Testing Program, president of the Council on Postsecondary Accreditation, and Executive Director of the National University Continuing Education Association.

STUDENTS OF THE THIRD AGE

Introduction: Negotiating the Retirement Rite

PAUL A. MILLER
President Emeritus, Rochester Institute of Technology

Learning in Elderhood

In an age anxious for educational reform, few if any responses exceed the importance of lifelong learning. A multitude of claimants press their desire for it on all manner of American (as well as, of course, other) institutions. And programs keep springing up in schools, colleges, universities, industries, voluntary associations, churches, private retreat centers, the special rooms of motels, and obscure corners of private and public buildings.

Steadily growing in both size and importance, the profession of continuing education serves to organize, direct, and monitor this educational revolution, whose sponsors find themselves as much transformed as the participants. Many continuing education leaders, including all of those who have authored this volume, reside in the very colleges and universities wherein lifelong education has garnered much of its legitimacy, as well as formulated the better part of its philosophy.

Students of the Third Age is a reflection on lifelong learning as sponsored by academic institutions. The book aims to extend continuing education to an already large and growing number of older people. Herein is lifelong learning linked to both human development and elderhood, the latter a stage encompassing the third and fourth quarters of the lifespan.

These practical essays, which center on learning in retirement (LIR), also introduce a genuine innovation: the member-driven Institute for Learning in Retirement.

Such ideas and their practical extension to elderly people respond, to a significant degree if only in part, to the aging of the American population. Thanks to medical technology and improved lifestyles, people can expect to live some 20 years or more after they retire from active work. By the start of the new century, close to a third of the population will be age 50 and above. More than 20 percent will be 55 and over. In the 1990s alone, the greatest increase—some 25 percent—will come to those who are more than 75 years of age. The authors see the development of a large learning force whose members may share in a zealous educational companionship.

From these trends, the authors derive a fruitful scenario. They provide hopeful glimpses of an elderly learning corps, and stimulate the reader to revisit the functions of education, work, and leisure. Out of this framework, then, comes in marked detail an account of how colleges and universities (and, by inference, other institutions) may serve the educational interests of the elderly.

There are surprising changes in the present cohort of elderly people from those that preceeded them. On the whole, they are not poor: In the last 25 years, the percentage of those over the age of 65 who live below the official poverty line has dropped from 30 to 10. More of today's retirees have already experienced continuing education, likely in support of their jobs. And a growing proportion of them have traveled, and enjoyed a range of cultural events. The influence of these changes finds them looking back at and revising what education, work, and leisure have meant to them. In their retirement years, many more of the elderly now are able to act upon these revisions and create life for themselves that is as fulfilling as it is unique. *Students of the Third Age* examines that expectation.

The revisions in thinking and practice are reshaping the traditional (one might say "canonical") pathway through life as practiced in Western civilization. A fourth of the lifespan goes to formal education, much of it related to the next stage—work, which accounts for about half of one's life. Finally there is the period after release from work that is commonly labeled "retirement." Leisure, seemingly present all along the pathway, has in fact long been the servant of both schooling and work. Traditionally perceived as free time, it was supposed to restore one for the return to classroom or job. Fusing and dominating economic and social values, this traditional pathway of life in Western pragmatic culture also ascribed personal identity: "What is it you do for a living?"

Over the past three decades this pathway has progressively undergone radical change. Formal education has extended beyond its early and concentrated period to invade the work phase, thus feeding the growth of continuing education. Thus learning has grown rapidly as an activity of "leisure."

These milestones—expanding education and changing the use of leisure—are vantage points from which one can look at both work and retirement.

This new thinking about education, work, and leisure brings to mind those times when work was subordinated to leisure. The ancient Greeks, for example, made leisure the fundamental aim of life. Leisure gave shape to personal destiny as a "calling" or the finding of a "true work." The Greeks built leisure upon learning, leading them to join the advanced reaches of debate, art, citizenship, philosophy, ritual, and music. More moral force went to leisure than to work, the latter for the most part done by slaves and women. To be sure, work in America still draws on a greater moral force than does leisure. But it is fair to speculate that leisure, no longer seen to be for restoration alone, now challenges the earlier balance.

Meanwhile, ever more rationalized and regulated in bureaucratic environments, work in America grows increasingly routine—first the work of industrial workers and, more recently, that of the more advanced and liberal professions. To weaker attachments to work (even a measure of alienation) can be added the distractions of an expanding popular culture. Thus, leisure becomes less the servant of work. As learning turns to an engagement with leisure, the latter takes on a more independent meaning. With their nature still emergent and muddled, modern retirees know something of the alterations in the traditional pathway, and react by applying new insights to their retirement years. To aid them is an aim of the LIR movement and its analysis, as follows.

Serving the LIR Movement

That learning in retirement may be thought of as an educational movement is but the reflection of the extent to which educational programs for the elderly are now fixed on the educational landscape. Their drama is exceeded only by their spirit of innovation—both qualities portrayed by *Students of the Third Age*. Some programs, like the remarkably successful Elderhostel, connect the learning interests of the elderly to educational institutions on a worldwide basis. Others, such as the Oasis Centers, are ventures of industrial firms. In addition, from a long and growing list of schools, colleges, and universities comes a dazzling assortment of community programs. Sparked by the growth in the numbers of, and changes in the outlook of, elderly people, the colleges and universities are now devising what is nothing less than a new educational form. It is capable of enriching both the way Americans live out their lives and, as well, the mission of the university. *Students of the Third Age* points to these potentials, and captures the drama of LIR as a new form and shows how to extend and sustain it.

The book spells out the formula for inserting an innovation into the fabric of a college or university. In one sense, this implantation produces a "college for elders." It is, at bottom, a university center made up of members who pay a fee in order to join, help plan the curriculum, give leadership to the courses, evaluate the outcomes, and participate in intellectual and social communities as products of the enterprise. The reader learns how the LIR center meets the developmental needs of its members, impinges on campus life, and enhances relationships and understandings between younger and older learners.

To be sure, the changes in education, work, and leisure all were influenced by the academy. Universities grew in popularity as they came to govern the process that certifies the credentials for most managerial, technical, and service jobs. They played a major part in professionalizing the middle class, and helped bureaucratize and routinize its occupations. Thus, LIR centers bring a measure of irony into colleges and universities. Influenced by new insights about creative leisure and given to self-directed learning, LIRs will doubtless challenge traditional methods wherever they may find them.

Imperative to matching the interest of LIR members to university activities is the schedule of reciprocities. On the one hand, the university may serve older learners as an oasis of quiet refuge and meditation. On the other hand, elder learners will seek to actively use the institution's intellectual, artistic, and recreational resources. Wise access to, and special uses of, campus resources will require the working out of reciprocal exchanges between the center's members and the parent institution.

The university may provide the campus as a new haunt, where older people may initiate and locate a chapter which features learning as a major component of creative leisure. Moreover, the campus can lend itself as the base (and support station) from which elderly people are able to launch forays into the local community which, with encouragement, turn into useful research and community services. It is not impossible to imagine, as elder learners grow in number, position, and influence on a campus, that suitable residential options may be designed and provided them.

Elder learners can return these favors with their own. With their special knowledge and experience, they may support the university in its teaching, research, and public service. If the opportunity to meet and learn with younger students exists, intergenerational learning is possible. Indeed, if done well and sustained, such a companionship might well transform the whole university environment. Those in elderhood possess more discretionary time, and this may be devoted to the achievement of university objectives. They also bring to the campus a myriad of contacts with the wider world. LIR centers may also stimulate their members to become patrons of the institution and, in time and with greater understanding, be motivated to share their material resources.

The campus interventions by LIR participants may well exceed the sponsor's expectations. A composite scenario of the LIR centers employed in this volume strongly hints at what is possible. To imagine such a scenario, one may picture a hypothetical Groverton University. It serves as an urban academic center of some 14,300 students and 2,500 faculty and staff. Five years ago, Groverton accepted the proposal from a committee of local citizens to create a Center for Learning in Retirement. The center has grown from 180 members in its first year to 478 members today. The annual membership fee is $250. Some 125 different members have led courses over the past five years, with 36 serving in the present term. In addition, 10 of these current course leaders and 28 other members collaborate with members of the teaching and research staff in pursuit of special interests.

Two years ago the "DeTocqueville Society" was organized to foster joint "student–member" projects in the community, and in so doing to widen understanding of the university. The society's last project assisted the Department of Police Administration, which had been invited to mediate a local dispute over police relations. The society organized and secured attendance at several community forums. Moreover, a committee of 17 members has recently organized and initially staffed a new foreign student center on the campus, and arranged its inaugural ceremony at Groverton's first "International Weekend."

The center's program for the current term has just gone to press: 34 courses with 383 participants; three receptions for new members; a term-end party; monthly meetings of the singles' club; and four weekend travel excursions. Requests are circulating for a show of interest in an international education tour of Mexico. The center's next newsletter describes a gift from the estate of the oldest charter member, who, having passed away eighteen months before, desired to endow a library on quality control in the College of Engineering.

As the reader of *Students of the Third Age* will discover, the Groverton scenario is underway in a growing number of colleges and universities. But, not unlike as at Groverton, their leaders and faculties may not fully realize that indeed a "college for elders" *is* growing up and into the institution's life. At an even deeper level, a new and influential idea is expanding and quietly enriching the perceptions held of the institution by the surrounding public.

It is an idea reminiscent of Ortega y Gasset's suggestion for centering the life, curriculum, and debate of the university. Gasset, the inspired Spanish philosopher and devotee of adult education, called this centering device a "faculty of culture." His assembly was composed of both a highly prepared professoriate and thoughtful leaders schooled in community affairs. Gasset's "faculty of culture" would vitalize the university as a civic institution and help sustain the debate on what makes up the public good. Moreover, the "faculty of culture," merging professional and civic disciplines, would stand as a model and source of stimulation for practicing the general calling of citizenship.

The lives of today's elders have encompassed much of a volatile century. The informed among them exhibit concerns about the American community, and many make deliberate plans to take on active community tasks in retirement. Inviting such people to the campus helps them hone and extend their skills, adding, at the same time, additional ways for the university to appreciate its own role as a civic institution. Improved public service is part of the idealism that informs the LIR movement and justifies its place in academic institutions.

This idealism is worth keeping alive! Colleges and universities vigorously concern themselves with worldly professions, corporations, and markets. But their stimulation of the civic community is more in doubt despite an academic campus in or nearby seemingly every American community. Older people, having lived through this evolution, are custodians and arbiters of a concern for community life. They may be a bit morose, and even express a tinge of guilt that the "rust of progress," as philosopher Robert Nisbet once called it (". . . increasing anonymity, displacement, and deprivation in the sense of organic relatedness to others . . ."), seems to have come on apace during the course of their generation, and particularly their maturity.

LIR participants often evidence a concern that they and those about them have come to feel ill at ease with government. They wander easily into discussions of what they see as a widening gap between experts and the public at large. Or they may exclaim over how government came to be perceived in their time as the surrogate for the broader and wiser action of citizens. Surely can they glance with nostalgia at the way things once were; but, more importantly, they plead for a recrudescence of those "small platoons" (to recall Edmund Burke) that spring from family and kindred groups, churches, service clubs, neighborhood associations, and those other local groups which altogether foster and depend on a primary citizenship.

With a meeting ground on the academic campus, elder learners respond naturally to still other needs that come from the intersection of community and campus. They have lived through two or three generations. Their memories record a long stream of events. This enables them, as they pursue a learning agenda, to fill in some of the blanks left by a faculty societal memory. Indeed, Americans rush so headlong into the future that the roots of their culture lay shallow in both the past *and* present. Strong and clear values and standards do not therefore easily develop. The result is often a tone of indifference (or but a short-term interest) to problems which affect public ends. Elder learners puzzle over these trends. In response, they show invariably a vivid and often competent interest in writing biographical tracts, family memoirs, and their interpretations of obscure events. While their children and grandchildren loom as the first beneficiaries of this effort, the university archives and the libraries of the community may also be considerably enriched.

The Retirement Rite

Whatever the reciprocities between a body of adult learners and the university become, elderly people will scarcely desire as their first objective to enrich the linkage between university and society. Instead, their explicit intent will be to study subjects which have been long-delayed. A more subtle intention will view further learning as a way to devise a new stage in their lives. Learning in retirement thus *helps* people to retire—an extraordinarily useful function, as the authors of this volume explain.

Even as the LIR centers help people to shift from work to a fresh stage of life, the process undermines the traditional meaning of retirement as that *chapter* in life which follows education and work. Rather, retirement becomes a *transition* or *passage* to such a chapter. It is a movement toward a "calling" in life, a grappling with "true work." Further erosion of retirement seen as a chapter rather than as a transition results from the new conditions of life for retirees. They have a good share of their lives yet to live; their health is better and they know more about how to sustain it; they are in a better financial position; they are better-educated; and many have experienced the concurrent practice of education, work, and leisure.

But for most, however apt their adjustments, few can free themselves from the grip of work life without feelings of tension and instability. Most retirees undergo a transition, with all the earmarks of a ceremonial rite, however early and adroit their plans. The LIR centers help one to navigate the transition. The centers also help turn tensions into useful guidelines for the lifestage to follow—creative leisure guided by continuous learning.

Among less distinctive others, three prominent markers appear along the passage through the retirement rite. *First:* Given more time and blessed with less distraction, the retirement transition encounters the finitude of life. However reluctantly, most retirees will engage in meditations on mortality. One datum is clear: On the other side of the new chapter stands death. Thoughts, events, tasks, and scraps of information once passed over lightly now return for a more earnest analysis. The mind turns to new questions: What happened in the past; what can happen in the future? What was accomplished in the past; what might be accomplished in the future? What is complete; what is not complete? These queries drift in and out of transcendental spheres which, surrounded by a hue of sobriety and honesty, make them broadly spiritual in nature. To face these realities and tie them up engages the meditative discipline; it will likely continue once the transition is over. Even dwelling on the past, no longer a sign of senility, serves to assess and summarize. To know and to understand the direction a life has taken, and to accept it, no matter how dissonant its notes might have been, helps the retiree to put it aside and turn anew to the design of the new chapter.

Second: Looking squarely at life's finitude and tying up the loose ends may be encouraged and advanced amidst the conviviality of others who are similarly engaged. These special developmental tasks of the elderly are eased and facilitated in the LIR environment. But the assurance need not stop there. With the casual and informal support of their peers, older people are (or at least may become) moral conservators. They can not only share historical insights but also express a seasoned faith in the future. They can demonstrate ways to overcome self-interest in action, and with such naturalness as to communicate with younger generations and serve them as a model. In behaving thusly, the elderly retiree invests in the affairs of young and old alike. And, once the transition to retirement is over, the practice may be sustained in a continuing companionship. These investments of self in a social context endure long after those who made them have passed from the scene. Sharpened in the retirement transition, and continued in a "true and good" work, they are investments that multiply and radiate outward to family, neighbors, and a widening community. This alone, it may be argued, can justify the LIR movement.

Third: The retirement transition also prompts the shift from instrumental to expressive values. To employ a different rhetoric, a new focus is made on sharing and improving inner strength, a greater emphasis on *being* rather than on *doing*. If the "third age" of adulthood is to bolster creative leisure, a finding of one's true work, a genuine happiness or contentment will assimilate into all that one does. What better helps one to reconcile and live with the inevitable impairments to physical health? What better than a full measure of enjoyment yields the felicity to accept mounting frailties, and to accommodate and use them in a full and expressive life? The "third age" learner, more free of duties to maintain one's self, can examine and build upon the strengths of an inner, personal being—some might say to enhance the soul. To redirect the balance in favor of expressive values will mean for some that they explore quite different social environments, thus bettering the odds that they may both strengthen and share their personal and expressive qualities. To this end the LIR centers, serving to integrate personal, intellectual, and social interests, offer an adventuresome pathway.

Crafting the Movement

The authors of *Students of the Third Age* help clear the way into educational institutions for some 40 million people who are either not far from or already in the retirement stream. This volume outlines how to meet the learning needs of this vast and still-new constituency. With the book's mastery, readers will know how to interest, invite, inspire, and organize these older citizens as self-directed learners on university campuses. The reader is virtually transported into the university milieu to see how this new class of learners may not only help themselves but, as a result, assist the university as a whole to better serve society.

As continuing educators, the authors exemplify a growing aspect of their field—the launching of new ideas and constituencies at the margins of their institutions, and (such being found worthy) the establishing thereof as permanent programs. In this manner their writings herein contribute significantly to educational research and development. Furthermore, the unresolved issues that this book recounts establish a veritable research agenda in such fields as education, academic organization, and social gerontology.

Indeed, while both the ranks of elderly learners and the numbers of responding projects are burgeoning, the authors suggest that more needs to be accomplished before LIR can be proved efficacious to all concerned. They are cautious and tentative about how the movement may impact upon society, and how the university may affect the elderly. Yet, while returns are not entirely in, the promise of these impacts and effects is clear.

Certain puzzles remain. Fortunately, however, the authors describe cases which carry the basis of clarification. For example, today's LIR centers more easily fit the interests of people from the upper middle-class world and its panoply of managers and professionals. Ahead is the task of making the LIR movement more inclusive as it unfolds in an interdependent and multicultural society.

Another question arises: In the end, how hospitable a sponsor will the university be? The LIR centers entertain a sizable number of experienced, articulate, independent-minded, mature people. Will their desires for self-direction stimulate or clash with a campus traditionally organized for the young? How plausible is intergenerational learning, and what might be its results? The authors probe the campus dynamic of LIR projects, and show the ways various colleges structure their programs. Clearly, there are many academic and institutional issues, concerns, and questions which must be addressed in establishing an LIR program.

Perhaps the greatest question surrounds the issue of what happens to people as they move through the retirement rite and into useful and enjoyable years of personal growth. To what extent can further learning be the organizing principle of creative leisure for those in elderhood? Will they be helped to manage the balances between the private and public dimensions of life? And between instrumental and expressive values? And what will college or university sponsors perceive in return, and how may *they* be changed in the bargain?

There is still much to learn of the LIR movement. But *Students of the Third Age* confidently leads the reader along a clearly marked pathway to doing just that.

PART I

The New Age Wave and Higher Education's Response

Higher education has a unique opportunity to join with older adults to find new roles for developing special purpose and meaning to later life, while at the same time enriching American society and its educational institutions.

1

Post-Retirement Learning

RICHARD B. FISCHER

America is becoming a society of healthy, active, and increasingly better-educated older adults. These older adults are significantly changing their expectations and view of retirement. More and more of them are finding meaningful use of leisure time through pursuit of structured learning in new programs offered by colleges and universities.

Until the past decade or so, the question of the continuing education of older adults—adults of retirement age—was more an issue for academic discussion than for educational practice. Post-industrial society in America had cast aside senior adults to make way for a youth-oriented economy and social system. However, the graying of America finally has caught up with its higher education system—or perhaps it is more that American colleges and universities finally are recognizing an important social reality. The definitions of a college student, and of what it means to go to college, are changing. No longer is the college campus a sea of young faces. There is a new creative and innovative spirit at work in higher education, focusing on opportunities to serve not only men and women in their twenties to fifties, but also a post-retirement study body aged fifty-five and older.

Emerging Demographic and Social Patterns

THE EXPANDING BASE OF OLDER ADULTS

Between 1990 and the year 2000, Americans 50 years of age and older will increase in number by 18.5 percent, to 76 million people. Those of ages 50–54 will increase by 25 percent, 13 percent of the population will be 65 and over, and those beyond 75 will increase by 26 percent (Ostroff, 1989). Figure 1.1 indicates a further breakdown of pertinent U.S. populations by age group.

Currently there are 40 million Americans over 60 years of age, and these persons can expect to live at least 18 to 20 years after retirement. And, this population concentrates in certain geographic regions. One-half of Americans over 65 years old currently reside in ten states: California, New York, Florida, Pennsylvania, Texas, Illinois, Ohio, Michigan, New Jersey, and Massachusetts (Bureau of the Census, 1989). Interestingly, while these states have the largest absolute number of over-65 adults, only three (Florida, Pennsylvania, and Massachusetts) are among the ten with the highest percentages of their population over the age of 65. The other seven in this category are Rhode Island, Arkansas, Iowa, Missouri, South Dakota, Nebraska, and Kansas.

These demographic changes, as well as several other significant trends, have caused researchers and educators to rethink the post-retirement life phase. Three considerations have resulted. *First:* Rapid and pervasive social,

Figure 1.1 ESTIMATED U.S. POPULATION CHANGE BY AGE GROUP: 1988–2000

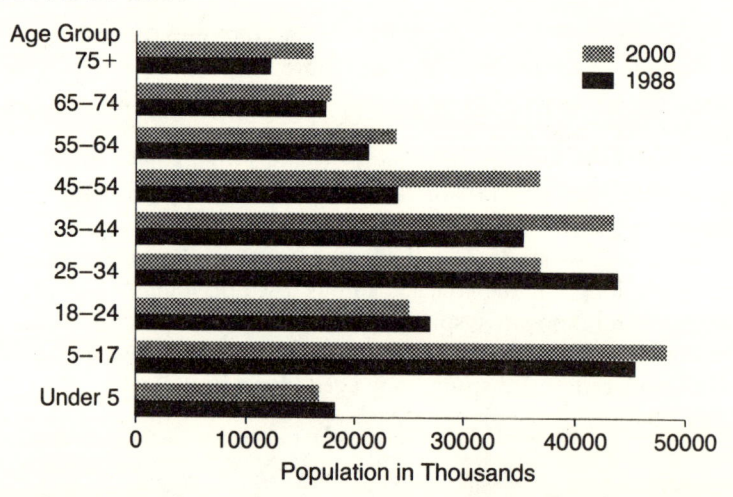

Source: *Current Population Reports,* Series P–25, No. 1018, U.S. Bureau of the Census, 1989.

technological, and economic changes have altered the relationships of all age groups to information, education, and lifestyle. *Second:* The nontraditional-age college student is no longer either unusual or unique. In 1988, according to the College Board, over 45 percent of the nation's undergraduate and graduate enrollees were already nontraditional—over 25 years old. *Third:* More and more people are retiring from "bright collar" jobs wherein they have been accustomed to using their intellectual powers.

In his book *Age Wave* (1989, xix), Dr. Ken Dychtwald points out that the coming "age wave" of older adults will challenge and shake every aspect of American society's dynamics, including education. With each generation of adults, lifespan, educational background, and the desire for intellectual stimulation and participation in lifelong learning activities increase. Today's and tomorrow's older adults are and will be healthier, better-educated, more active, and more affluent than those of any past generation. This population, which has been nicknamed the "chronologically gifted," or OPALS (Older People with Active Life-Styles), will seek, if not demand, that higher education institutions respond to their learning, cultural, and social needs. In effect, higher education is becoming a direct care provider for older adults instead of only providing training for care givers in custodial roles. If the university is to live up to its responsibilities as a collegial institution, it *must* include older adults as full members of its student body.

MORE AFFLUENT AND BETTER-EDUCATED

A growing number of Americans are retiring more affluent than their predecessors. About 59 percent of retirees aged 55 to 65, and at least half aged 65 to 74, are "comfortably retired" with incomes at more than twice the poverty level (Longino, 1988). Even more rewarding to those concerned with higher education's role is the improvement in educational background of older adults. In 1980, only 28.3 percent of those 55 and over were high school graduates. By 1990 this had increased to 49.4 percent. By 2010, over 55 percent will be high school graduates (Bureau of the Census, 1989). Never before has such a large, growing, and educated proportion of the American population reached retirement age.

THE CHANGING WORKFORCE AND THE FAMILY UNIT

The increase in retirement-age persons will also exacerbate dramatic shortages of workers in the American labor pool. Areas in the Northeast, Middle Atlantic, and older industrial states, and labor-intensive fields such as education, health, and retailing will need to seek ways to attract and train older adults for a host of new entry-level positions. The declining stability of the traditional family unit, increases in the divorce rate and single-parent households, and a rise in the number of two-profession families also will shape attitudes and options toward the role of retirement and retirement-age family members in today's society (Queeney, 1990). All of these changes will increase pressures on the higher education system to develop new models to serve the educational, survival, coping, giving, learning, growing, and enjoyment needs of older adults (Wigdor, 1989).

A NEW VIEW OF RETIREMENT

While shifting demographic patterns underscore the potential "market" demand developing from those of retirement age, it is not demographics that determine who is "old"; it is stereotypes and attitudes that determine old age. Today's senior adults are creating new models of what is elderly. It is the change in their expectations for *quality* of life rather than mere *length* of life that is the most dramatic: Older people are changing their expectations about what it is *like* to be older. Those approaching the "golden pond" years also are thinking differently about themselves, and (as part of that mode of thought) about becoming older. They are choosing to be more in charge of their own lives and more mentally and physically active (Stern, 1989).

Having discovered the buying power of older adults, media no longer portray them as forgetful, doddering, inactive, or unattractive. These (and many other) negative stereotypes about them embedded in American culture are changing. Dychtwald (1989, p. 49) sums up this new view of older adults in commenting "Tomorrow's older people will have little in common with yesterday's. They will have traveled to more places, read a greater variety of books and magazines, met more people, lived through more world changes, experienced more sexual and lifestyle experimentation, lived longer . . . than any previous generation in the history of the world." No wonder that retired adults are choosing to redefine their post-retirement "leisure" years by seeking more active and intellectually interesting uses of their time. As Laslett (1989) points out, retirees no longer are "old people" in the traditional sense. Historically, Americans have been viewed as progressing through only two active periods or ages of life before retirement. The first age, childhood and adolescence, generally ended with the reaching of one's majority (or the completion of high school or college). The second age was focused on work—earning a living and looking toward retirement as a period of leisure, modest comfort, and slowing down. Today, many adults entering retirement are *not* slowing down, but rather beginning yet another active phase of life. They are the new members of the Third Age movement, a French term stemming from Les Universities du Troisieme Age, which was begun in June 1973. The Third Age is one beginning with retirement, when a person seeks personal fulfillment, takes up new skills, and/or extends cultural horizons.

EDUCATION AS LEISURE

More and more older adults are finding meaningful use of their leisure through pursuit of a structured learning experience. Continuing education is one of several ways in which they can achieve self-growth.

Older adults tend to seek out those learning experiences which either increase their control over their own lives or help them with their personal or social identity (Courtenay, 1989). Studies have indicated that they prefer to take courses that provide a sense of meaning (anthropology, philosophy, religion) or the ability to cope (health care, science, languages). Of course, other than intellectual curiosity, the strongest motive for older adults' participation in education is the desire to establish vital new social connections, to feel needed and wanted, and to have a really good reason for daily human interaction.

WHAT IS HIGHER EDUCATION'S RESPONSIBILITY
IN THIS CHANGING ENVIRONMENT?

One can view education for older adults in much the same way as education for youth. It is an investment in society. It is consistent with an American higher education philosophy of equality of opportunity, of access by students from all classes and origins. It is also consistent with higher education's fundamental role and responsibility of knowledge creation and dissemination.

Colleges and universities have at least four major responsibilities to post-retirement learners. *First:* Just as colleges work with younger generations to help them understand the values and importance of the past, they have an equal role in helping older generations to understand the values, culture, and technology of today.

Second: The emergence of the "young elderly" has brought to light a significant group of people who can continue to participate in society after retirement. Higher education must act as a catalyst for mobilizing these people for productive roles in society for their 20 or 30 years of life after retirement.

Third: Colleges and universities have a responsibility to foster diversity in intellectual, cultural, and social life by educating students of all ages about aging and ageism. This can go a long way toward helping change the attitudes of a youth-oriented society wherein stereotypes of old age have been so negative.

Fourth: Higher education has the responsibility of fostering the effective use of society's limited resources by reducing older adults' need for health and social services. Mental stimulation has a positive correlation to improved physical health and well-being. Learning increases the strength of nerve transmission and changes the physical properties of cerebral nerve endings. Studies also correlate the maintenance of mental vigor with the capacity to survive (Winter, 1986). Overall, there is increasing support for the notion that lifelong learning can be an important life extender.

Aggressive response of higher education to these responsibilities will help older adults to create and shape change, and to obtain more control over both their lives and their environment.

Higher Education Responses

There already are many gerontology centers and schools where aging has been dealt with as a clinical issue. But, by and large, except for alumni "colleges," higher education response to the learning needs of older adults is a recent phenomenon. Although institutional programs for learning in retirement were established as early as 1963, a University of Wisconsin–Milwaukee study (Heath, 1989) has shown that the growth of programs was slow until the mid–1980s. Historically, new systems of education frequently have emerged in response to changing social needs. For example, in the period of early American enlightenment, Benjamin Franklin brought curricular issues to public discourse through library discussion and presentation debates. In the last third of the 1800s, when new levels of agricultural and industrial competence were needed, the land-grant system of colleges and universities was developed. Development of community colleges and the adult community school concept flourished in the early and mid–1900s in response to greater numbers of first-generation college students and increased demand for wider community involvement in the educational system. More recently, new instructional and nontraditional education systems have been implemented by higher education institutions to meet the growing needs of part-time adult students. Now a new learning mode, the member-driven Learning in Retirement (LIR) "institute" model, has emerged to meet the needs of older retirement-age adults.

MEMBER-DRIVEN LIRS

While described in detail in the next chapter, these programs, sometimes called "senior colleges," "academies," or "institutes," are referred to here under the generic heading of learning-in-retirement programs, or LIRs. In these programs, the older adult members determine their own curricula, teach their own courses, administer and market the program, and engage in self-governance under the aegis of a local college or university. The programs, generally self-supporting, are located on a college campus and function as intellectual cooperatives. Every member contributes and few people, even faculty, are paid. A 1989 survey by the National University Continuing

Education Association reveals the existence of more than 161 different member-driven programs for older adults in the United States.

Although these LIR programs represent the newest and fastest-growing educational mode, interest in serving the older adult is, as we shall now see, broader than just "senior colleges."

TUITION WAIVER PROGRAMS

Tuition waiver programs (free, state-funded, or reduced-tuition for older adults) are perhaps the most common. Older adults are permitted to attend regular classes on a space-available basis. Peterson (1987, p. 47) points out that whereas more than 18 states have legislated tuition waiver programs, they are not widely used by older persons as yet. (A notable exception in this category is the "My Turn" program at Kingsborough Community College in New York, with over 2,300 participants.)

ELDERHOSTEL

Perhaps the most well-known and successful example of an educational program for older adults is Elderhostel, a Boston-based nonprofit organization that offers short-term residential courses under its own name in cooperation with local colleges. Over 1,300 participating institutions worldwide serve more than 165,000 older adults annually.

In 1988, Elderhostel established a national coordinating office to begin a new program initiative to broaden its mission beyond its established residential model. Known as The Institute Network, this initiative focused on the LIR model to provide noncredit, college-level course work on a nonresidential basis in a local community setting (usually on a college campus) with the assistance of Elderhostel in planning and implementing the program. As of August 1991 there were 80 institutes affiliated with the network.

OTHER MODELS

Programs such as the University of North Carolina's Center for Creative Retirement, and Grant MacEwan Community College's "Senior Studies Institute" in Canada, are pursuing grant-funded research on the impact of shifting populations of retirees, and on the development of wellness, leadership, and outreach humanities programs for seniors. Plans are underway to launch intergenerational learning projects at many schools, and conference and research centers for older adults have been built in California and Delaware and are under construction in North Carolina.

Other innovative programs have been started by some colleges and universities in order to meet specific and somewhat narrower needs of older learners. Senior Ventures programs at Southern Oregon State College, Weber State College, and Central Washington University merge travel, learning, and vacations on college campuses.

Of course, serving older adults is not strictly an American phenomenon. The Universities of the Third Age movement (initiated, as we have seen, in France in June 1973) now encompasses over twenty different countries on four continents. The present version is a broad-based approach to research and service for the purpose of seeing what universities can do to improve the lives of older adults.

Distance learning strategies also are being introduced to serve older adults in geographically or socially isolated locations. Pioneers in this area included the Seniors Education Center at the University of Regina, Canada. Their program, entitled "Prairies Visionaries," serving over 1,800 participants in six locations spread over 450 miles, offers one-way video and two-way audio courses.

All of these providers are learning that several basic andragogical principles appear to apply across the adult lifespan (DeRenzo, 1990): Older adults have the need for self-direction. They are driven by intrinsic motivations, such as self-esteem and creative expression, rather than by extrinsic factors. Working in partnership with the elder culture requires different skills from the usual task orientation of an adult educator. This age group will exaggerate issues of individual differences. There are increased differences in physical, cognitive, and social development. It is more difficult to predefine norms. The participants can be fiercely independent, with little tolerance for bureaucracy. Truly, the instructor or program coordinator involved with the teaching of older adults must become a facilitator of learning—not the designated "leader" or "expert."

How is the future role of postsecondary education likely to unfold in the area of education for older adults? The answers will be as diverse as the cultures and locations of the institutions themselves. What is increasingly clear from the growing body of research in a number of disciplines is the positive correlation between the educational activities of older adults and their subsequent and prolonged physical and psychological well-being. In our aging society there can be no doubt about the scope and magnitude of the need for older adult educational programming. Nor can there be any doubt about the growing public endorsement from the students of the third age for those many institutions addressing this need.

Issues and Questions

Educating older adults has its detractors. Development of LIRs raises a number of complex policy and philosophical questions. The issues revolve around questions about who should be educated and for what purpose, who decides on who is served, how a successful program is run, what the resource needs are, and what the implications for age-interpreted or age-segregated learning are. These and other issues are dealt with in the following chapters.

Higher education institutions have a great deal to benefit from the establishment of an LIR. Not only does the institution gain materially from both short-term and long-term revenue and bequest flow: An LIR also can be a strong academic center for the study of the humanities, a nexus for the development of intergenerational programs, a source of volunteers on the campus and a complement of eager participants in university events. LIR members, most of whom will not be alumni of the sponsoring institution, develop the same loyalty and identity as the institution's own alumni. Too, LIR members can provide a wealth of expertise to the college, from fund-raising to patent research, and are excited about the possibility of continuing to contribute their professional talents. LIRs in such states as South Carolina have become magnets for economic development by attracting affluent retirees.

LIRs also can become starting points for research into the theories of life stages, demographic trends, psycho-social issues, human service delivery systems, and economic issues facing older adults. These activities will give support to an emerging field of educational gerontology.

In the tripodal scheme of higher education (teaching, research, and service), LIRs satisfy at least two of these missions by combining the traditional roles of teaching and service. LIR members teach in service to themselves as a study body, and also in service intergenerationally. For example, the KAT Program in Boston provides meaningful roles for older adults in meeting tutoring needs for latchkey teenagers (Keller, 1983). The University of Delaware uses LIR members to teach in the school's freshmen reading sessions—an artful combining of life experience and teaching.

Conclusion

LIRs represent a new learning structure that increases older adults' sense of well-being, productivity, and dignity, and at the same time allows society to benefit from the experience of men and women with a rich personal history. It is becoming evident that there is a well-educated group of older adults who expect higher education institutions to provide learning programs for them in both special contexts and open classes. LIR programs can offer older learners the opportunity to be an integral part of the teaching–learning transaction.

PART II

Developing Successful College-Level Programs for Learning in Retirement

The task of initiating and maintaining a member-driven LIR can be made easier with practical and pragmatic suggestions derived from the experience of others. This section helps identify pathways to success.

2

LIR Program and Organization Models

KENNETH E. YOUNG

The member-driven learning-in-retirement programs are emerging as a new educational model at many colleges and universities. While individual programs have unique features, all models have some common characteristics revolving around issues of membership, fees, privileges, staffing, curriculum, and organization. Emphasis is not on doing for older adults, but enabling them to take responsibility for their own educational development within the framework of a university or college.

This chapter focuses on those educational programs (particularly member-driven programs) that are organized as centers or institutes serving older persons in the local community. These programs vary greatly in title, location within the institution's table of organization, administration, structure, curricular formats and subject matter, size, cost, fee arrangements, and physical location, and in almost every other way imaginable. Despite their great variability, however, these learning-in-retirement programs (LIRs) can be usefully grouped into two general program categories: institution-driven and member-driven.

Institution-Driven Programs

These are programs designed, controlled, and run by a college or university (usually the continuing education division). The institution customarily conducts some sort of community needs assessment to determine the shape and size of the "market." It often organizes a small advisory group consisting of some older alumni and community leaders in the area. Then a program of course offerings is developed, a brochure is prepared, and a promotional effort (primarily direct mail) is launched. The program is usually managed by a paid college staff coordinator, drawing on other institutional personnel as needed. The courses ordinarily are taught by regular (or on occasion adjunct) college faculty, who are usually paid an honorarium consistent with that given for teaching other continuing education courses.

One of the most successful programs of this kind, "My Turn," sponsored by Kingsborough Community College, offers credit courses, and many of the participants are working for academic degrees. "The College at 60," sponsored by Fordham University, is another example.

Member-Driven Programs

These are programs that, although sponsored by colleges and universities, are organized on a membership concept. The programs may start because a group of older persons approaches the institution with a proposal, as was the case at American University, or the institution may take the idea to a group of retired persons in the community, as happened at the University of Delaware. In either event a written agreement is established, bylaws are developed and approved, and the organizing group, working with a designated paid staff member from the institution, proceeds to develop a program and recruit other members. In some instances faculty members help to plan and teach courses, but in most cases the curriculum is developed and the courses taught by the members themselves. The courses almost always are noncredit.

The oldest program of this kind in the United States is the "Institute for Retired Professionals," founded in 1962 at The New School for Social Research. The largest is the "Institute for Retired Professionals and Executives" at Brooklyn College, with over 2,300 members.

What are the advantages and disadvantages of an institution-driven program versus a member-driven program?

A program directed by professional staff of the college or university usually is more efficient, relates more comfortably to the rest of the institution, and can avoid possible problems that might arise with an active membership group. Rarely, however, is a professional staff member assigned full-time to this responsibility, at least during its early years. The most common arrangements are: (1) a mid-level professional (ordinarily in continuing education) who spends one-third to one-half time coordinating the program for older persons, and the rest of his or her time with other programs; or (2) a part-time professional (perhaps a former full-timer who has cut back because of family responsibilities or who is beginning to phase into retirement).

The tendency is to add one or more full-time clerical staff as a program grows—but it often has to get to be quite large (800 or more students) before it supports a full-time professional director. Of course this sort of staffing arrangement does not assure that high-level, constant, understanding attention will be given the program. Furthermore, the participants in the program tend to be somewhat more passive and limited in their involvement than are students in member-driven programs; often they just take their courses and go home. There are, however, a few large programs wherein students, with institutional encouragement, have developed quite an active schedule of social and cultural activities.

Member-driven programs, on the other hand, depend on the quality and commitment of their volunteer leaders, and the situation therewith may vary from year to year. A domineering or lackluster chairperson can have an adverse effect on a group, especially in its formative period. Also, as is true with all member-run organizations, about 20 percent of the members do about 80 percent of the work, and their efforts can be very uneven. In addition, a membership group takes on a life of its own. As can be the case with student body governments or alumni associations, an organization of older persons may develop an operational style, or group expectations, that will conflict in some ways with the sponsoring higher education institution's.

On the positive side, a membership arrangement offers participants a much-needed opportunity to become involved in a meaningful activity, makes it much easier to develop a social network, and can build a strong commitment to both the program and the institution. This approach also is more likely to assure that the program responds to the members' wants and needs, since they design it themselves.

Finally, because much of the work of the organization, often including the teaching of courses, is done by volunteers, the program can be more cost-effective. Members do a great deal of volunteer work for the program, such as recruiting new members, assisting with registration, organizing special events, planning the curriculum, producing the catalog and the newsletter, and helping out with typing and other chores. They also are willing volunteers for other activities in the college or university. They participate in fund-raising phoneathons, serve as conversational partners for foreign students needing help with the English language, work with counseling staff as resource persons on career opportunities, and so on. These intergenerational activities are discussed more fully in Chapter 9.

As the numbers of older adult students on campuses continue to increase, it is expected that colleges and universities with free or discounted tuition, or special services for older adults enrolling in regular programs, eventually will move to or add one or the other of the approaches described above. Also, when these programs grow in size, it is likely that the institution-driven programs will tend to become more like the member-driven ones (as the students propose new ideas, organize to carry out various activities, and volunteer to assist with administrative details), and the member-driven programs will tend to become more like institution-driven ones (as more paid staff members are added and policies and procedures are embedded in place).

Common Characteristics

Most successful LIR centers or institutes have certain common characteristics which could be used to describe them. A model might emphasize the following eight basic descriptors.

1. Is designed to serve the learning needs and interests of older adults located within commuting distance of the program.

2. Has as its major purpose the offering of a broad-ranging educational program, a substantial part of which would consist of college-level learning experiences.

3. Is sponsored by:

    • an accredited college or university;

    • another institution or organization working in collaboration with an accredited college or university; or

    • an institution or organization judged to be sponsoring a program comparable to those found at accredited colleges and universities.

4. Is nonprofit, charges a relatively modest tuition or membership fee, and has a need-based scholarship program.

5. Publicly commits itself to affirmative action goals.

6. Utilizes volunteer teachers or course leaders who are members of the LIR.

7. Offers social, cultural, and physical experiences that complement the curriculum and are appropriate for the program participants.

8. Provides for meaningful participant involvement in planning, evaluating, teaching, and (where appropriate) administering the program. Participant involvement is usually in the form of:

    • an advisory group that meets regularly with the program director, or

    • a membership arrangement.

It is useful to elaborate on these basic descriptors.

ORGANIZATION

The variations in programs range from virtually no organization at all, except for a typical student–institution relationship, to a highly structured arrangement. Most programs over time do tend to develop either formal or informal systems that permit the students to participate in course development and evaluation, and in the organizing of complementary activities (trips, speakers, social events).

Member-driven programs, of course, by their very nature, call for: (a) a "charter" from the institution, which may simply be a letter authorizing the program and establishing its authority and responsibilities; and (b) bylaws which set forth the purpose, functions, and structure of the organization (see Appendix I).

The relationship between a membership organization of older adult students and an institution of higher education is in many ways quite similar to that of a traditional student government and a college or university, but there also are some important differences. For example, the older adult group does not require the guidance and oversight that must be given undergraduate students, and the older adult group probably has a greater capability for generating volunteer services and additional financial support for the program.

The most important issue—the nexus between the program and the rest of the institution—especially comes into play in spelling out the role of the key institutional paid staff member working with the program. No matter whether a program is institution- or member-driven, staff/member relationships can vary considerably. There are institutionally run programs wherein some, if not all, members are heavily involved in decision-making; membership programs where, despite all the democratic apparatus, the director really rules the roost; and just about every possibility in between.

The paid program director or coordinator is a key element to the long-term success of a program. In a very real sense, that person serves as the dean of a small college, with its own recruiting, admissions, registration, record keeping, and curriculum. He or she must: (a) be respected by and have access to other major decision-makers in the institution; and (b) understand that the staff person is working for the college or university, with the consequent responsibility for assuring adherence to institutional policies and procedures; but (c) also appreciate the unique and often sensitive nature of the relationships required in dealing with older adult students seeking more than additional education.

Programs may be located in the continuing education unit (the most common arrangement), the school of education, or elsewhere within the institution. No one "home" necessarily is better than another. It is important that the program fit comfortably within the institution's mission, and have the enthusiastic support of the president of the college or university, and that adequate space has been provided. One program, the "Institute for Learning in Retirement" at American University, lost its campus space in 1989 and has had to become an independent legal entity affiliated with the university but renting classroom space in a nearby church.

ELIGIBILITY

Most state laws and institutional policies providing for free or reduced tuition for older students require that participants be 65 years of age or older. College and university programs based on a course or membership fee vary from specifying no age (like the "Metro-East Institute of Lifetime Learning," at Southern Illinois University–Edwardsville) to stating different ages—50, 60, 65. Many programs, however, appear to be flexible about applying an age cut-off, allowing a younger spouse or a younger disabled-retired person to participate.

None of the programs surveyed in a 1989 study by the National University Continuing Education Association (Appendix III) had a specific participation-time or attendance requirement. In fact, the more established membership groups have some members who join for the year but might be gone for several months—say to Florida for the winter, or on an extended trip. Many of the programs do "take roll" in classes, but primarily as a means either of assessing the popularity of their offerings or of identifying members who might be ill.

Although a number of programs have names such as "Institute for Retired Professionals and Executives," in practice they have not ruled out other white-collar (or even blue-collar) workers or housewives. Most do not even require a college degree or high school diploma, but rather emphasize that a person should have a desire to learn. The "Temple Association for Retired Professionals" at Temple University, for example, admitted to membership a retired tailor who had not graduated from high school but had read widely. He eventually became a course leader, and then was elected president of the association. Again, even where programs have specified credentials, exceptions often have been made.

Several programs call for an interview as part of the admissions procedure. At the aforementioned "Temple Association for Retired Professionals" the director conducts interviews. Other programs have assigned this responsibility to a committee. The "Academy of Senior Professionals," Eckerd College, conducts an interview by a committee on membership, followed by a review and final action by the organization's senate. "The Plato Society," UCLA, has a membership committee that interviews all candidates, accepting about one out of ten. The purposes of the interview apparently are: (a) to answer questions so that prospective members understand what kind of program they are joining; (b) to identify and discourage persons who might be senile or otherwise unable to participate effectively; and, most importantly, (c) to stress the importance of member participation in the program.

FEES

The "Senior Adult Education Program," at Centenary College, Louisiana, the "University of the Third Age," at Asnuntuck Community College, Connecticut, and the "Open University" program at Virginia Commonwealth University, charge no fees. The Virginia Commonwealth program uses free locations around the city of Richmond, and volunteer instructors, and the university picks up administrative costs. At the other end of the spectrum, the previously cited "Academy of Senior Professionals" at Eckerd College (in Florida) has charged a $1,000 initiation fee (which can be paid on an installment plan), and $50 in monthly dues. Most programs with annual membership fees cost between $75 and $300 a year. Programs based on individual course registrations charge anywhere from the full rate for noncredit continuing education offerings, to a discounted rate (usually half), and even to free courses on a space-available basis.

Programs based on individual course fees explicitly promise only the course for the fee (although some brochures mention the possibility of group-organized social activities). Programs with membership dues usually list a variety of membership benefits.

CURRICULUM

Most programs follow the standard format of two terms a year—fall and spring. However, the terms usually are shorter than the collegiate 15-week semester, 10 or 12 weeks being more common. UCLA's "Plato Society" has three 14-week semesters. Some programs have shorter mini-terms. Classes typically meet once a week, except perhaps for courses such as foreign languages (which often meet more frequently). Classes ordinarily run 1½ or 2 hours, with a short break, and vary from large lectures to small seminars and studio groups. Most members prefer classes that offer an opportunity for discussion; some like to give reports or lead discussions. Too, a number of programs have a few between-term activities, such as a lecture series, a film series, or study tours.

In most programs the kind of courses offered are quite similar to those in the institution's regular credit course curriculum, with a strong emphasis on the social sciences, the arts, and the humanities. There is less interest in mathematics and the sciences. A few practical courses, such as financial planning and the stock market, attract interest. However, members do not like classes focusing on the problems of older persons ("Coping with Aging," "Grieving," etc.) and most programs shun the kinds of activities found in senior centers (bridge, macramé). Where the university or college faculty members teach the courses, they usually adapt their regular courses to both a shorter time period and the particular interests and richer backgrounds of older students. Where LIR members lead study groups the program may be constrained by the kinds of expertise available from within the membership, although the fact is that the resources usually are surprisingly diverse.

Many programs have a curriculum committee to design the curriculum or to advise the staff on this matter. The "Institute for Retired Professionals" at the New School for Social Research has one of the most elaborate curriculum development systems. A member interested in leading a study group must post the topic and attract other members, who sign up. That group then meets to design the course, and the proposal is submitted to the curriculum committee for approval. When a course is approved and listed in the catalog, members are selected to run the course. If something were to happen to a group leader, another leader would be selected by the group.

In these programs there are no tests, usually no homework to hand in, and no grades. The result is that older adults easily overcome any fears of failure and can relax and just enjoy the learning experience.

FACULTY

Most institution-driven programs use paid faculty or teachers, in contrast to membership programs in which members serve as volunteer (unpaid) teachers or discussion leaders. Membership programs often make an effort to involve institutional faculty as guest speakers and resource persons. Many programs also have a special lecture series, drawing on faculty or distinguished persons in the community.

Programs differ in styles of teaching and the sizes of classes. Programs utilizing regular paid faculty tend to have larger classes and to use a lecture format, although there are some exceptions to this. Member-led classes usually, but not always, are restricted in size and emphasize a seminar approach. As programs grow they tend to develop a variety of formats, including lecture–discussion combinations, team leaders, coordinators with a group of visiting lecturers, and the like.

When paid faculty members are to be used to teach a program, the staff member (or another representative of the program) approaches the prospective instructor, and also seeks approval of the appropriate academic department. If volunteers are to lead study groups, they usually are interviewed by members of the LIR curriculum committee to determine whether they know their fields, appear to have teaching skills, and are aware of the unique aspects of working with older students. Seldom are these volunteers' credentials submitted to academic departments for approval.

Regular faculty usually are paid per course. This payment may or may not parallel the amount paid for either overload or continuing education instruction at the institution. Volunteers are not paid, although some programs give them a discount on the membership fee; and one program (the "Institute for Learning in Retirement," American University) provides complimentary memberships for new course leaders. Because they are receiving "free" services, some programs are reluctant to impose any strong standards or requirements on volunteer leaders. Evaluation of courses and volunteer instructors often is done very informally, or is used only to help determine whether to repeat a course. In most cases not enough is done to orient course leaders and to work with them to help improve their teaching, although the "Academy of Lifelong Learning," University of Delaware, has initiated a faculty development program for its volunteer instructors.

STUDENT STATUS

Some programs (for example, the just-mentioned "Academy of Lifelong Learning," University of Delaware; the "Open University," Virginia Commonwealth University; the "Temple Association for Retired Professionals," Temple University; and the "Center for Learning in Retirement," University of California–Berkeley) are located at sites away from the main campus. Therefore, the participants have less opportunity to take advantage of any privileges that are provided to regular students. Some institution-driven programs, such as "My Turn," Kingsborough Community College, provide full college-student privileges. Most such programs, however, limit student benefits to those available to part-time continuing education students; financial aid and health-center services usually are not provided.

Membership programs that have a comprehensive rather than a per-course fee issue student identification cards, usually the same as those given continuing education students. These cards entitle holders to many campus privileges, including the right to check books out of the library, discounts at the campus store, access to certain facilities, and free or discounted tickets to social and cultural activities. Institutions that follow this latter policy have found that the older adult students help to fill out audiences at events (art exhibits, musicals) that may not attract large numbers of undergraduates. (These students may even sit in on such activities as dissertation defenses and moot courts!) They also prove to be regular patrons of the campus store and dining room.

Unfortunately, many colleges and universities still continue to see full-time undergraduate students as their primary, predominant clientele when in fact a considerable number now have more part-time than full-time students, and more older than younger students. Institutions are being encouraged to review their policies and procedures in light of these changing conditions. Students aged 65, 75, and even 85 represent potentially valuable additions to the campus, and should be treated as first-class citizens. The case can best be made, however, when older adults pay the comprehensive (rather than the per-course) fee.

SOCIAL ACTIVITIES

Events such as receptions, luncheons, and dinners almost always are self-supporting. Some programs have established small funds, using gift monies or income from certain activities that might be tapped to pay for some social events, such as welcoming coffee hours for new members, or refreshments at open houses.

Member-driven programs seem to have more social activities than do the institution-driven ones. And older, larger programs do more along those lines than do newer, smaller programs. Social events are seen as an important aspect of these programs. They help to welcome newcomers, foster acquaintanceships, build a sense of collegiality, and communicate the values of the program. There are limits, however, to what can be done. Many program participants are reluctant to go out in the evening, and/or do not have their own transportation. In most programs, students tend to come to the campus only one or two days a week; thus social events must be scheduled so as not to conflict with classes.

CULTURAL ACTIVITIES

Program participants are involved in three kinds of cultural activities: those organized by the program itself, those sponsored by the college or university, and those available in the community.

Program-sponsored cultural events include the publication of student writings and drawings (such as at the "Institute for Retired Professionals," The New School for Social Research), guest speakers, film series, student exhibits, recitals, and plays. The full range of these activities is more likely to be found in the larger, well-established programs. The events usually are free.

Colleges and universities have a great variety of cultural activities, and almost all of them are accessible to program participants free of charge or at a student or senior-citizen discount. In addition, many students are active attendees at community cultural events. They often participate on their own, getting together informally, but on occasion organize a group under the auspices of the program. Everyone pays his or her own way.

SIZE

Programs vary in size from the 50 members in the "Retired Executives and Professionals" (Manatee Junior College, Florida) to the 1,800 at the "Institute for Retired Professionals and Executives" (Brooklyn College). The "Academy of Lifelong Learning," University of Delaware, at 1,400 and the "Temple Association for Retired Professionals," Temple University, at 700, are two of the larger programs. The "Institute for Retired Professionals," New School for Social Research, has capped its membership at 630 and has a waiting list.

Where programs have set a ceiling on numbers of participants, the reason almost always has been space limitations rather than policy considerations. A case can be made that when enrollment grows beyond a certain level (exact number usually unknown), a program may begin to lose its cohesion, but this issue is complicated by the fact that students tend to come to campus on various days of the week (there may be a Monday group, a Tuesday group, etc.) and to take certain kinds of classes (current events, foreign languages, etc.), so that their friendships are more likely to emanate from these relationships. Even with as few as 100 or 200 participants in a program, some students may not know one another. Policy considerations aside, the facts are that most programs find it difficult to say "no" to applicants when there is space available and when additional participants help to keep fees down and make it possible to enlarge the program's offerings. Also, it is *very* difficult to establish and administer a fair and equitable policy for limiting enrollments.

An even more difficult policy issue has to do with class size. Most students prefer seminar classes that permit active participation. The ideal size for discussion groups is about 15 students ("The Plato Society," UCLA, holds to that limit), but financial considerations and enrollment pressures tend to push the numbers upward. Except for classes limited by needed facilities (art, computers) and teaching methods (foreign languages), the tendency is to keep increasing class size in response to student interest. ("The Institute for Learning in Retirement," American University, gradually has increased class size from 15 to 30.) This is a particular problem with a course that becomes very popular, usually because of the teacher. A course in anthropology at the "Academy of Lifelong Learning," University of Delaware, regularly attracted 150 students—cut off at that number because of room size.

Setting limits on class size is a matter of guesswork. If 25 students are admitted to a course, only 20 or 22 may show up for the first class, and there always will be a certain number of absences (usually different students each time). While the program is very important to the students, it is not always the most important thing in their lives. When grandchildren have birthdays or friends come to town, those interests may take precedence. Also, there are the inevitable doctors' appointments, illnesses, and other absence-causing matters of import.

Deciding on minimum class sizes also can be a problem. As long as there are rooms available, most programs with volunteer teachers allow classes as small as five students. With paid teachers, the required registration must be sufficient to cover that cost (usually 12 to 15 students). A related issue is the number of courses for which participants are allowed to register during a given semester. Most programs do not limit the number; however, some do because of space limitations. Other programs charge extra for more than two or three courses. Again, it is hard to administer a fair and equitable way to limit enrollment. The reality is that most older adult students will ignore administrative limits and go to the classes of their choice.

FINANCING

Programs do need to be subsidized during their start-up period (about three years). In most cases the sponsoring institutions have provided the underwriting, although some or all of the costs could be covered by an outside group such as a foundation, a corporation, or a wealthy donor. Such funds are raised by volunteers helping to organize the program, coordinating their efforts with appropriate institutional personnel. Even if external funding were available, however, it could be argued that the college or university should assist with program development as evidence of its commitment to the program. If a program is well-managed, it should be able to meet all of its costs, direct and indirect, by the fourth year of operation. During the early period of development, the institution's support usually comes in the form of providing free facilities, the partial time of a staff member, and other kinds of support services like preparation of publications.

Public institutions, in the past, have been slow to push these programs into a completely self-supporting mode, viewing them as an effective form of community relations; but that attitude now seems to be changing as state and federal funding diminishes. Private colleges and universities, always deeply concerned about the balance sheet, increasingly are moving toward the philosophy that programs must be self-supporting. These changes translate into a policy whereby programs either must pay all operational costs *plus* an overhead charge of anywhere from 25 to 55 percent, or they are charged for each specific service (such as rent, telephones, and computer time).

A program that does not pay its teachers has limited paid staff costs (one or two personns), which is the largest budget item. Therefore, 100 members at $300 a year, 150 at $200, or 200 at $150 would produce $30,000 in income, which should be sufficient to cover operating costs.

Programs that have been in existence for some time have begun to receive unsolicited contributions and occasional bequests from members. Some programs have developed policies and procedures for soliciting and accepting such gifts. Of course, efforts in this area *must* be coordinated with the institutional development office. More details on financing may be found in Chapter 6.

Conclusion

Although the primary purpose of college and university educational programs for older adult students is to provide opportunities for continuing learning, the most successful programs also respond effectively to certain powerful social and psychological needs of this constituency. Such programs can provide retired persons with an important (to them) purpose in life, offer opportunities for developing new relationships, and, most significantly, allow them to continue to feel that they are still in control of their lives. Many of these educational programs can and do touch on the first two needs, but the third need requires that institutional personnel not have an attitude of "doing for" the students, but rather seek out ways to allow and encourage the students to do for themselves.

Institutions of higher education that sponsor LIRs are responding to an important and growing educational–social need. As was mentioned in the preceding chapter, there are many potential benefits therefrom to the institution. Most importantly, however, LIRs serve as model programs, presaging the future of higher education. They represent unique forms of organizing, of utilizing different approaches to teaching and learning, and of serving a nontraditional student clientele. In sum: Colleges and universities can learn a great deal from the LIR concept.

Author's Note: Much of the material in this chapter was drawn from a paper based on campus visits, reviews of catalogs, and telephone interviews, which was prepared by the author for Elderhostel.

3

Starting Your Own Learning-in-Retirement Program

MARK L. BLAZEY

Linking the resources of an institution of higher education with a group of eager older learners may seem like a natural event, but the process must not be undertaken casually. Balance is a key. Balance will be needed in combining the institution's mission, goals, and policy with the older adults' need for self-determination. Balance will be needed between the social and academic focus of the program. Balance will be needed to create a physical, psychological, and learning environment which meets the needs of older adults.

This chapter presents practical suggestions to help establish a successful member-driven, university-related program designed to provide intellectual and social stimulation for older adults, and to alert organizers to some pitfalls and questions commonly encountered in developing such a program.

Programs of this type repeatedly have proven to be immensely rewarding for both the participating older adults and the higher education institution and its officials. A university-related member-driven organization of older adults can produce a level of synergy exceeding that of either the university or a group of older adults alone. To ensure that this mutually beneficial synergy develops it is critical, when considering starting such an organization, to plan for the striking of a balance between the mission of the university and the goals of the group. Mission and goals *must* be complementary.

Universities traditionally have provided services to older adults which have been quite similar to those provided to all other students. The university has decided which courses would be of interest to adults, and offered them to senior citizens either free or at a reduced rate. As with most standard university courses, the interests or requirements of students have not played a major role in determining course offerings or content. For purposes of this book, that type of offering has been defined as university-driven—because it is based on what university professional staff and faculty believe students "should" receive.

Member-driven programs, on the other hand, are developed specifically to meet the interests of the older adults, who alone determine what sort of courses they would like to teach, as well as which subjects they would like to study. In the classic adult education philosophy, adults assume responsibility for their own learning. A model of self-determination emerges not unlike that of such other member-driven groups as fraternal, social, and church organizations, reading groups, and travel clubs.

Linking the learning resources of universities with groups of older adults who desire continued intellectual stimulation may seem to be a natural event. But, like many other entrepreneurial activities, it requires a champion within the university, and a small group of dedicated older adults who can mobilize the community.

The Preconception Phase—Positioning for University Commitment

Because obtaining the commitment of the host university is crucial to the success of the program, the approach to university administration should not be undertaken casually. Universities by-and-large are extraordinarily deliberative; the process required to create a new degree program or a new course of study is lengthy. A series of hierarchical committees review plans, taking many months to reach conclusions about whether the program is sound. Only then does program implementation begin.

Some learning-in-retirement programs have failed to get off the ground because senior administrators at the university have been presented with a traditional program request and a formal analysis of the merits of spending money to fulfill a community service need. Demographic trends, community need, and the responsibility of the university to provide a community service are rarely as persuasive as a group of 40 to 50 older adults banded together and driven by the desire to establish a university-based member program to meet their social and intellectual needs.

The first step in the process is to identify a champion from within the university, a person who shares the desire to establish such a program and is able to commit some university start-up resources. A director or dean of continuing education is a typical university champion. In other cases it has been the institution's president, or the spouse of a trustee.

The Conception Phase—Keep the Message Simple

When launching a program for older adults it is critical to have the vision of a new program in mind and be able to express that vision in terms that will excite the imagination of those who might like to participate. Exciting the imagination of people who have lived more than half a century, traveled extensively, held important posts, and been involved with the community may not be an easy task, but doing it is the second step toward a successful program. Older adults are, in general, quite sophisticated. Most, by their own account, have heard it all before. Many have sat through thousands of lectures, seminars, workshops, and classes and have found them less than exciting and fulfilling. They also have no tolerance for bureaucracy, and a university bureaucracy can be especially vexing. They *must* be insulated from it and given the freedom (within broad constraints) to manage their own program.

What makes the LIR programs successful is that, since they are based on the imagination and energy of the members, they are relatively unencumbered by "normal" bureaucracy. If potential members have the opportunity to feel the spirit and enthusiasm that these programs generate, they will be eager to join.

What is the best way to stimulate and excite sophisticated adults? It is *not* likely to be any of the following: reading a newspaper advertisement; opening bulk mail to find a flyer for yet another educational program; academic course listing in a university catalog; a 30-second burst on drive-time radio; or a public service announcement on television.

What does generate excitement is associating with dynamic, interesting members of the community and learning from their personal experiences and insight. Excitement comes from opportunities to meet and make new friends and to be exposed to new ideas. Excitement comes from fulfilling the desire for social interaction as well as intellectual stimulation. This excitement becomes a very powerful and unique feature of university-related member-driven programs for older adults because the university provides a natural environment in which to bring the forces of socialization and intellectual stimulation together.

The third step in forming a learning-in-retirement program is getting people together to talk. One of the most effective ways to do this is a series of small luncheon meetings. After the first couple of meetings, the university champion or designated staff person coordinating the program will have secured the volunteer commitment of several older adults who share a vision of the excitement and power of this type of program.

This small core (of say from four to ten people) will provide the nucleus for building the program, and will become the temporary steering committee. One of these people should be designated as group leader, but this should not be a university employee. The leader pro tem calls planning meetings and provides thoughtful guidance to drive the process forward. Another volunteer member of the steering committee should focus primarily on curriculum—that is, on identifying respected members of the community who could serve as course leaders to provide the crucial intellectual stimulation on which the success of the program depends. The third critical assignment for one of the leadership group should be communicating the message to the older adult community (the traditional marketing function). A fourth person should focus on the social aspects of the organization and the range of activities, which might develop from purely social to purely academic. Finally, someone needs to start thinking about finances. This ad hoc group provides not only the leadership, communication, and planning for the program, but more importantly the infectious enthusiasm to push it ahead.

Gathering a Critical Mass of Community Support

Once the leadership group is identified, which should take no more than a couple of weeks, the members should begin to develop a larger critical mass of support. One way that has been used effectively with new programs is to invite prospective members to small, informal meetings or "coffees" where the ad hoc leaders deliver an enthusiastic message. Some LIRs have used testimonial video tapes and/or slide shows which capture the experience and wisdom of those who already have started programs. One of the best video tapes of this kind features Edwin Buxbaum, an octogenarian and founder of the "Academy of Lifelong Learning" at the University of Delaware. The twenty-minute tape is available from the University of Delaware through its Division of Continuing Education.

From each group of about a dozen participants in these small meetings, three or four will be enthusiastic and want to participate immediately. After sponsoring from eight to ten such meetings, a critical core of 20 to 40 people should exist to supplement the initial organizational group as the founding members.

The First Trappings of an Organization

From this group of 20 to 40 interested members, the next step is to select an advisory group. Members of this group should be chosen for their ability to garner a broad base of support within the general community, as well as to influence the academic community. The success of the program and the speed with which membership grows will be related in part to the characteristics of this first advisory group. Ideal initial members include retired teachers or faculty; retired politicians; members of community service organizations such as hospitals, charitable organizations, or other civic groups; and highly visible retired newspaper reporters, editors, or television personalities. Members of the first advisory group should be selected because of the resources they can leverage, either personally through a commitment of time and work on behalf of the new organization, or through the contacts they have in the community and their ability to influence others to join.

Initially, members are attracted to the program largely through word of mouth. Friends telling friends has consistently been the primary means of recruiting members to this new type of educational and social organization. Obviously, if the first members of this group have limited contacts in the community, the membership will grow slowly. If however the first members have diverse contacts throughout the community, then membership will grow more quickly. It is important to remember that the initial advisory group and the core group of founding members will establish a tone and image which will guide the mission, program, and membership of the organization for years to come.

Space—the First Frontier

Without a specified place to meet and call its own, the organization is handicapped. Space usually is a precious commodity, a scarce resource at higher education institutions. To acquire space requires a critical mass of influential people, another reason why simply stating the need for the program is not as effective as showing the names of those who already have joined *in anticipation of a place to meet*.

The best space for this type of program is that which promotes easy interaction among the members, and so rooms for both learning *and* socialization are important. A number of programs begin with space allocated in a university conference center, an old house which has been given to the university, or off-campus facilities which are not fully utilized. Willingness of the LIR group to renovate an older building may be a key to obtaining such space. Classrooms spread across a 400-acre campus or throughout a 10-story building will not promote the social spirit that is so essential to the success of the program. Providing dedicated space for this group is one measure of the importance the university places on the needs of this group. Universities will also make older adults feel wanted by providing access to the facilities normally provided to all other students. Usually they will not avail themselves of these regular student facilities, but they feel good because they do have access. The affinity that the older adults feel for the university will be directly related to their perceived treatment by the university. Space and access to facilities are very important variables!

The Program

Obviously, linking the organization for older adults to a higher education institution implies strong intellectual rigor. But neither intellectual rigor nor social programs alone are adequate. Successful programs for older adults design a continuum of activities which range from purely social or recreational to academic. In addition to the formal academic courses, many programs offer such semi-academic activities as lecture or enrichment series during lunch, and afternoon special-interest speakers.

Social activities range from purely "for fun" parties and dinners to study/travel trips. Special-interest groups often form in response to the needs of particular members. A singles group that meets monthly is one example, and tennis, hiking, and canoeing outings are popular others. The balance between social and academic activities is always left to the direction of the group, but most groups provide diverse activities to attract and keep an interested, enthusiastic membership.

Membership Dues

Invariably, one of the early issues that arises deals with budgets, costs, and membership dues. Price and financial considerations usually have emotional undertones which relate to the responsibility of the college and the higher education institution to provide community service programs. Many believe it is the responsibility of the college or university—particularly the *public* college or university—to provide these programs *at no cost* to the older adults, and sometimes they may be right. Usually, however, members pay dues to help cover the costs of the program. Most existing programs are expected to operate on a financial break-even basis, including payment of employees' salaries and rent for facilities. In any case, the best approach to determining fees is to begin by preparing a comprehensive budget in an attempt to identify the costs (see Appendix V). And, right from the first, don't be stampeded into setting a fee because it "feels right." Start by acquainting all the founding members with the *real* costs of the program.

Even if the university has a mission to provide community service consistent with the mission of the member-driven program for older adults, it is still critical to identify budget costs, because no university has an unending source of funds. Whether the costs are covered fully by the university or the individual members, ultimately funds dedicated for these purposes must be allocated among competing priorities. A public institution with funds set aside for serving this population may decide to cover all the costs and require no membership dues. A private university which is funded mainly by student tuition may be compelled to pass along all of the cost of this program to the users. Otherwise, tuition-paying undergraduate and graduate students would have to underwrite the cost.

STEPS TO DETERMINE THE DUES
STRUCTURE TO ENSURE SELF-SUFFICIENCY

Budgetary details are covered in Chapter 6; however, several observations made there are pertinent to this discussion of the start of a new program.

It is extremely difficult to change the dues structure once it has been established! There is an almost visceral reaction on the part of older adults to any increase in cost, no matter how small or how well-justified. Therefore, it is very important to project costs as accurately as possible in the beginning, thus avoiding the pitfalls of underestimating. Also, in order both to ensure a long life for your program and to make sure it has a solid financial base, immediately consider increasing the budget estimates by 15 to 20 percent. And one last word to the wise: Don't set the initial fee too low, and don't rely on either external or internal subsidies for operating funds.

Political Support

Another dimension of support that is crucial to the success of any new venture is political support—not partisan politics but the political support that comes from people with influence who support the program. For example, one college president started a program because he felt it would be beneficial for his mother (and others like her). Having a program that met her social and intellectual needs obviously would have the continued support of that president.

In another case, the members of one long-standing LIR program were chagrined that the university did not appreciate their contributions to the university community. After all, they spent a considerable amount of time volunteering to help students needing remedial tutoring, yet they enjoyed no support from the top. Not one member of that program had a personal tie to the president or any member of the board of trustees; no members of the board of trustees participated in the program, and no member of the older adult group was prominent in the community or had connections which were likely to influence the thinking of any administrator at the university. Therefore, the program was constantly fighting a frustrating battle for recognition and appreciation. The university, on the other hand, lost an important opportunity to gain the support of hundreds of older adults.

The president and trustees of the institution should be involved in the program from the beginning. Consider making them honorary members, and make sure they receive LIR communications on a regular basis.

Volunteer Structure

Nearly all older adults have two traits in common: many years of experience, and the willingness to volunteer their time to help others. Volunteerism is an integral part of LIR programs. In the case of member-driven programs for older adults, interest in volunteering is directed from within the organization. Members who volunteer to help run the program provide not only a source of able and important workers to help the program meet its goals, but also an opportunity for the members to feel of value through their participation.

Creating an effective core of volunteers to support the LIR is ongoing hard work. Do not expect volunteers to come in, look around, see what needs to be done, and do it. Volunteers need to be recruited with specific tasks in mind, tasks that should be meaningful and well thought-out. All of the support needed to complete a task should be ready and waiting for the volunteer's arrival. Since a frequent mistake is not structuring the volunteer tasks, a comprehensive list of such jobs should be developed, with responsibilities identified for each. This should be compiled in a book available to all who may wish to contribute.

Volunteers should come in prepared to do a specific job, not left to their own devices. Continued interest in volunteering is directly related to the benefit that the volunteer perceives he or she is adding to the organization. Volunteers who arrive and find nothing meaningful to do soon stop coming. It can take months to build a strong volunteer network, but it takes only days (or even hours) to destroy it. The volunteer chairperson is the lead volunteer who provides direction for all participants. Do not expect a paid staff member to be as successful as a volunteer in attracting a core of working peer volunteers.

This discussion is not intended to undermine the importance of full-time paid professional staff. Every successful volunteer-based organization has at least one full-time paid staff member, who acts as the glue that holds the operation together. The successful volunteer chairperson, however, leads by example.

Role of Course Leaders/Peer Teachers

One of the most powerful features of member-driven university-related programs for older adults is the practice of peers teaching peers. Unlike traditional university programs, successful member-driven programs do not create a hierarchical class structure wherein teachers are members of the ruling class and learners are relegated to a lower-class status. Much of the power of the member-driven environment is drawn from the fact that *everyone* is a learner and contributes fully to the intellectual cooperative. There is equality in the teacher–learner transaction.

Many organizations have given considerable thought to the title they assign to members who lead the learning. Titles such as "faculty," "teacher," and "instructor" carry connotations which may set them above the rest and work against the concept that each person is responsible for his or her own learning. The title of "course leader" or "class facilitator" has a participative connotation which is more conducive to any egalitarian concept of adult learning.

Initial Publicity

Although word-of-mouth has proven the most effective way of encouraging older adults to join member-driven organizations, in the end spoken words alone are not enough. A member-driven organization that has yet to run its first course can establish credibility with a well-planned brochure. Such a brochure need not be expensive. In fact, "slick" brochures frequently do not send the right message. But the other extreme is also true: A typewritten, "home-grown" newsletter does not help to establish the credibility of a fledgling organization as one capable of offering quality programs and services.

A publication bridging these extremes ought minimally to be eye-catching, prominently displaying the name of the organization and its founding members. Names of the initial steering committee (if such help to establish credibility) are also important to include. The names of, and a very brief description of, the first course leaders and their courses will explain better than anything else what a new member can expect in terms of both course quality and course content. Descriptive words which promote "newly renovated" facilities, "renowned" course leaders, and "continued intellectual stimulation" in a warm, friendly social environment nicely promote the program's intentions. Careful planning of the first publication will make subsequent membership efforts all the more successful. Chapter 5 provides a more comprehensive analysis to guide marketing strategies.

Converting Inquiries into Members

It is important to remember the value of both social stimulation and continued intellectual development in making an LIR successful. The reason that luncheon groups work so well to establish the first core of interested members is that they bring people together socially to discuss an intellectual endeavor. While it *is* true that a certain number of members will agree to join simply because a friend asks them to, that method of recruitment has its limits. And recruitment based on presentations to civic groups and other organizations encouraging membership are not even that effective, because they discuss abstract principles. Personalize the program, and people join.

One of the most consistently effective ways to encourage initial membership is to get prospective members out to meet the course leaders (who then talk with them about LIR activities) and other current members of the organization. In so doing, prospects are brought together in a social environment similar to what they are likely to experience once they become a member. The message that comes through this process links the social aspects of the program with the intellectual stimulation thereof. The bottom line is that it is important to create the kind of physical and psychological environment that demonstrates to potential members the spirit and enthusiasm they are likely to experience when they join the group. This is the best way to allow them to see for themselves, *before* they sign up, rather than be forced to rely on the word of a well-meaning but possibly off-the-mark acquaintance, and be disappointed later.

Quick Membership Growth

One method for encouraging members to join at the program's inception builds on the concept of "founding members." These are, in the truest sense, special members who have (and demonstrate) the insight and confidence to imagine how an organization of this type can enrich their lives and the lives of others. They do not have to experience it to understand the possibilities. In fair return, they should be recognized for the effectiveness of their contributions and enthusiasm.

Many other people, even if somewhat lesser lights, like to be among the first to join an organization so that they may be considered part of this special group. Early recruitment can be enhanced by letting those members know that they will be considered part of the "founding member" (or "charter member") core and recognized by means of—for example—a prominently displayed plaque. It is however important to realize that ordinarily quite a few individuals who choose to become founding members will not continue as "sustaining members." About 25 percent will drop out after the first year, and each year thereafter. Nevertheless, the credibility of an organization cannot help but be enhanced by establishing itself as a large, fast-growing entity early in its life. The challenge, therefore, is to provide a program so stimulating that individuals who joined initially to be part of an elite group of founders end up staying because the program meets their needs.

It is also important to recognize the efforts of the long-standing sustaining members. Lists should be prepared and prominently showcased of members who joined at the beginning and have maintained their membership without interruption. Also identify members who have belonged for enough years to be of note. As the organization grows and matures, be very sure to keep careful records about the membership patterns, so that these long-term members may be properly recognized.

Governance Structure

During the early stages of development (especially), it is helpful to have a small core of dedicated people willing to commit time and energy to organizational structure. Initially, four critical leaders will be needed: a chairman, and individuals responsible for curriculum, membership, and social activities. Each of these four will in turn create a supporting structure managed by committee chairs and committee members. The example of organizational structure in Figure 3.1 demonstrates the committee structure that emerged to support the major activities that members felt were the most important. Similar structures appear in virtually all member-driven programs.

BYLAWS

Any democratic organization must have written procedures governing the major aspects of its operation. These procedures are variously referred to as constitutions, charters, or bylaws. One of the early subcommittees of any new LIR will focus on the creation and establishment of bylaws. Finding a set of generic bylaws dealing with a program that has similar concerns, missions, and goals helps make this process much easier. Appendix I is a sample of bylaws which can be used as a model.

RELATIONSHIP WITH HOST INSTITUTION

The relationship that develops between the host university and the member-driven program can assume some characteristics of a classic parent–child relationship. Universities desire to be nurturing and supportive while at the same time the older adults seek independence and freedom of action. As with parents and their children, the relationship is delicate. Be ready to deal with the control that the university must exert in order to administer its fiduciary responsibility and budget control. But also be ready for the older adults' strong demand for autonomy, which can manifest itself in a classic "we–they" syndrome that tends to frustrate cooperation and communications.

In order to minimize this tension, careful nurturing and open communications are essential. Establish mutual operating expectations early on. (Sometimes this must be done in written form—see Appendix VI). Since budget control seems to be the most sensitive area, involve LIR members in

Figure 3.1 Typical LIR Committee Structure

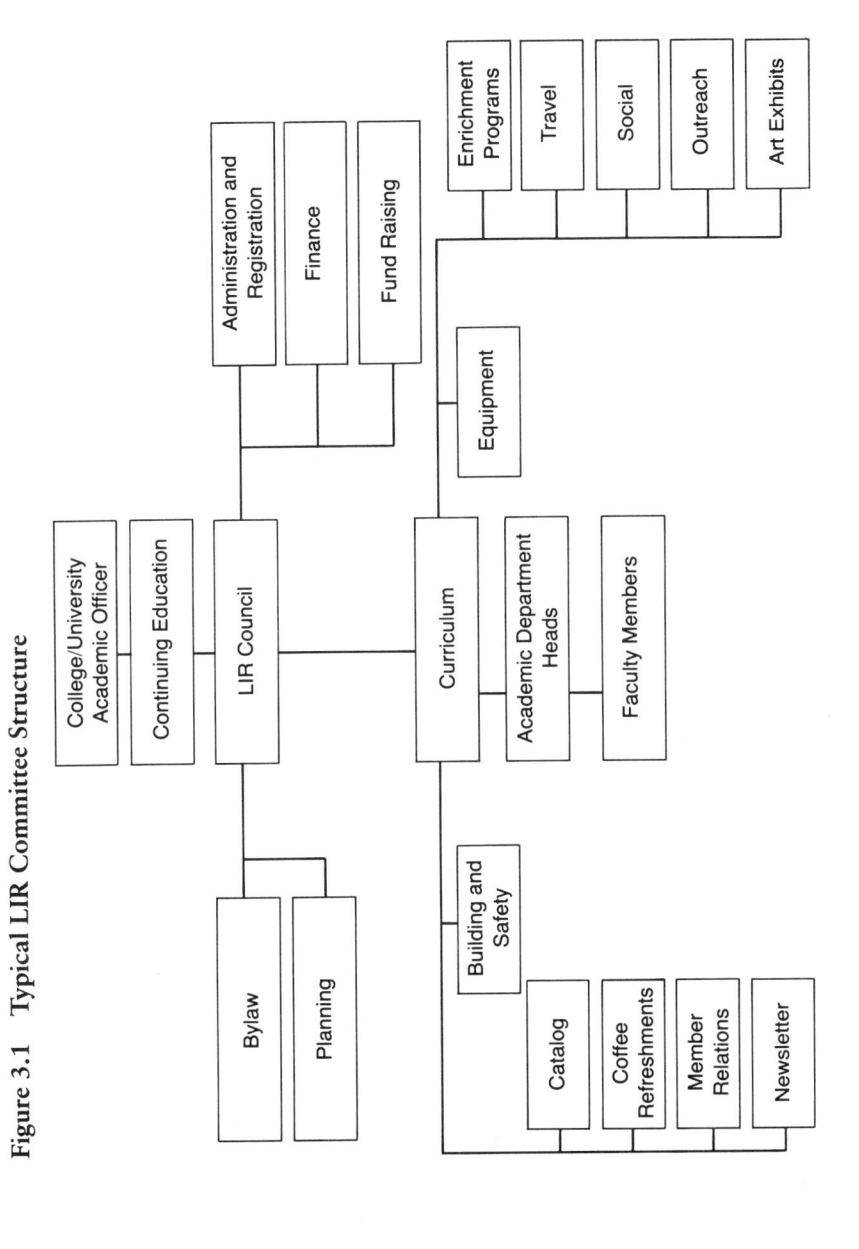

budget decision-making. Identify budget categories that the LIR group can control. Establish broad spending boundaries based on expected revenue, and delegate spending authority to LIR members within these categories. Relationships between the institution and the LIR membership will almost certainly be smoother as a result.

HISTORICAL RECORDS

One role in the governance of the organization should fall to a historian who will methodically maintain records on the evolution of the organization. Brochures, goal statements, writings of members, photographs, and newspaper articles all will form the nucleus of a story that is being repeated throughout the United States. It is of considerable future value to have a member take on the responsibility of gathering and sustaining your version of that story through the years of the organization.

COURSE EVALUATIONS

Sooner or later a group of members in the LIR will propose a systematic method of evaluating the courses offered. Once this is proposed, consideration needs to be given to what to do with the results and, indeed, how important those results are. (What happens if individuals participated in a course and didn't like the leadership? How does one fire a volunteer?) Harvard University ran a comprehensive series of evaluations for its learning-in-retirement program and then decided that the best use for those evaluations was to line the wastepaper basket.

While sponsoring institutions must be concerned about maintaining the educational integrity of the LIR, its members will of course share the same concern. They will not participate in an intellectually bankrupt program. Older adults know better than anyone else what they need and like, and what is quality instruction, and they are perfectly willing to vote with their feet. That is, they simply won't attend another class led by a weak course coordinator or presenter. Normally, if a class is not fully subscribed (or, worse, if no one attends), it does not run. Problems with good and bad classes take care of themselves in volunteer organizations run by members. Several LIRs have even begun faculty development seminars to enhance the teaching skills of the peer leaders.

Details Too Small to Mention

The title of this section may look foolish, but in this writer's searching for tips on starting and running LIR programs a number of small details came to light which by themselves did not warrant a paragraph. Put together, however, they provide insight into some questions, issues, and sensitivities which could be useful to LIR coordinators.

- Planning for the future, though crucial, is hard for older adult members. Be aware of the sentiment expressed by the late congressman from Florida, Claude Pepper, and shared by many LIR members: "I don't even like to buy green bananas." Short-term commitments are more easily made than are long-term.

- Make sure that room lighting is bright, since visual acuity is diminished for older adults.

- Expect higher-than-normal energy costs, because there is a lower tolerance for cold rooms in the winter and hot rooms in the summer.

- Be sensitive to the presence of outside noise. Due to gradual hearing deterioration, ambient external noise more easily disrupts classes.

- Ensure accessibility for adults with impaired mobility. Do not let physical barriers prevent potential LIR members from participating. Also, be sensitive to minor problems (e.g., loose carpet) that could pose a hazard to members.

- The wants and needs of LIR members probably will far exceed the expectations of the new LIR coordinator. It is hard to imagine the demands that will be made, and it is equally hard to foresee the personally satisfying rewards that can come from meeting them.

- Facilities and amenities are crucial. But don't underestimate the power that a simple luxury like a bouquet of fresh flowers can have on the human spirit. The LIR should have a warm and welcoming physical environment, even for dealing with intangibles.

- Colors influence attitude. Bright, cheery tones worn by the coordinator improve the morale of LIR members. The same is true of decor: The smallest touches of color can have a big effect.

- Many LIR members live alone. Taking the time to memorize members' names and personalize the welcome brightens their day. Many LIRs provide name tags to help people get to know each other.

- Coordinators should be sure to *listen*. Overheard conversations help the coordinator to connect people with similar interests, and can aid in identifying future leaders. For example, in overhearing a conversation, one learns that an LIR member likes photography. Cultivating that interest, the coordinator arranges for the member to create an exhibit. In no time the shutterbug may be teaching a popular class in photography.

- Coordinators *must* possess a high tolerance for ambiguity and frustration, and have great patience. Too, they must be able to subjugate their egos to those of the LIR members. Through all this (and more), coordinators create an atmosphere that meets the needs of members and makes them feel delighted with the program. Delighted members in turn make the program grow by telling and recruiting their friends.

- The coordinator must be trained in the use and minor maintenance of instructional (audiovisual, or A-V) equipment. Do not expect this support from most LIR members.

- Remember that LIR groups aren't fond of rules. Many perceive rules as "advisory." Others perceive them as "optional." The best rule a coordinator can follow is to give priority attention to the members. Remember that, unlike any other continuing education students, LIR members represent an *organized* constituency with the knowledge and experience to use their collective powers to achieve their goals. And many of them socialize regularly with trustees and other influential members of the college or university community.

- When it comes to signing up volunteers, remember to recruit more than may be needed. And expect wide variability in their contributions. Some could run the world. Others have trouble handling themselves.

- When planning an event, expect more people to attend than your "sign-up" lists indicate.

- Every LIR activity should have secretarial support.

- Expect unexpected problems, and be willing to fix anything.

- Be prepared for emergencies, including heart attacks, strokes, seizures, and fainting. Medical emergency, technical, or CPR training may help save a member's life.

Conclusion

Given the diversity of programs, higher education institutions, and the needs of older adults, it is impossible to cover all of the variables that will affect the new program. The best advice, beyond the information in this book, is to make contact with some of the organizations throughout North America that have similar interests. Chances are good that they will be experiencing the same types of problems or concerns that you face.

Appendix IV provides a list of programs for older adults and institutions sponsoring LIRs. This list can serve as a basis for networking with other organizations.

4

Instructional Program Design

HENRY T. LIPMAN

While it is recognized that learning is a social as well as intellectual experience in LIRs, the curricular philosophy should be the basis of instructional decision-making. This philosophy encompasses decisions on the level of academic rigor, mix of the course contents, and instructional format. Central to this discussion is the extent of volunteer peer teaching—using the best among equals—versus the use of professional teachers.

Curricula development in member-driven LIRs is based on the intellectual and leisure-time interests of the members. With retirement and increasing age, members' needs and desires for continued intellectual challenge and growth have not diminished, but the content focus has. Now intellectual interest is no longer on vocationally oriented topics, as it was in most of their adult life. Rather, it is directed toward the humanities, liberal arts, and social sciences.

In the LIR, members select either subjects of current interest, or those which had a long-time appeal but could not be pursued because of career and family pressures. Their interest in these topics is indeed serious—but not so serious that they want to become experts. Rather, it is to understand the major characteristics and broad implications, and not the minutiae. In brief, LIR members favor survey-type programs.

While members want courses and study-groups of consequence, they also want them to be free from the pressures of examinations or testing.

They are looking for a permissive environment, one in which they can carry out the requirements of the program but still can feel free to try new ideas. Many members also favor programs to which they can bring insights gained in their work careers and life experiences. They want to contribute to the learning process; to share with others the special ways of looking at events or information that varied experiences have given them. To accomplish these aims, the role of discussion is emphasized in almost all groups.

In designing the curriculum, members readily accept—and all LIRs take into account—the mission and philosophy of their college or university sponsor. Differences in mission and philosophy are reflected in how one LIR differs from another in balance between academic and leisure-time programs, the subject matter of study-groups and courses offered, the level of academic rigor required in the classes, and the nature of course leadership.

These are the boundaries that shape the educational design of most LIR programs. Within the framework of the sponsoring college or university's mission and philosophy, study-groups and courses are created to meet the interests of the members with maximum opportunity given them to provide input into (and otherwise contribute to) each of the programs. This chapter provides the basic elements that make up that design.

An Overview of LIR Programs

The many learning interests of member-driven LIR participants are reflected in the wide range of study-groups and courses organized by the members of each program. In both large and small LIRs, the programs include a core group of courses and classes in the humanities and liberal arts, with literature, history, public affairs, and music and art appreciation among the most popular. These are frequently supplemented by foreign language classes, and workshops in painting and writing. Some of the larger programs include in their curricula recreational programs such as bridge, group singing, and chess; and skills and craft programs ranging from fly-tying to creating with beads. Many sponsor folk-dancing and physical fitness programs, and some have "fun" groups in which members work together to solve math, logic, and language puzzles.

Adding to the range of educational opportunities available to members is the agreement by (most of) the sponsoring colleges and universities to grant members library privileges and allow them to enroll, without cost, in noncredit continuing education classes, or to make such classes available to members at a reduced fee. In a number of instances, arrangements are made for members to enroll on a free or lowered-fee basis in university credit or new-career programs.

In many of the LIRs, the academic offerings are augmented by travel programs which the LIR organizes. These normally include one-day or overnight bus trips to museums, to places of historical significance, or to a nearby city to enjoy its cultural offerings. In some instances LIRs will organize and sponsor (either alone, or with other units of their own university, or with other LIRs) two- and four-week overseas study tours. The recent development of the Elderhostel Institute Network, with its emphasis on overseas study programs limited to Network members who have prepared for the programs in their own LIRs, will expand the number of members involved in overseas studies and travel.

Coupled with these educational activities are the largely informal social programs carried out by all LIRs. These include a community lounge (most often with coffee available, to be sure), where members can get together before, between, or after classes; periodic rap sessions; brown-bag luncheons; end-of-term and mid-term class parties; annual dinners or luncheons; and, of great importance when available, a cafeteria where members can have lunch together.

In general, the number of courses and classes that an LIR will conduct is determined by the size of the membership. Thus, Johns Hopkins Institute's "The Evergreen Society," with about 75 members, has some 10 courses and classes, most of which are in the liberal arts but also include recreational and travel programs. A typical mid-size LIR, the 300-member "Renaissance Society" at California State University–Sacramento, schedules 20 to 25 programs each semester, with emphasis on the liberal arts but also including courses in computer technology, word processing, foreign languages, writing and painting (workshops), and a forum series for which university faculty members and community experts are the speakers.

The nation's largest LIR, the "Institute for Retired Professionals and Executives" at Brooklyn College, with over 2,300 members, offers more than 80 courses (14 in literature alone), with others on such topics as Encounters with Science, Folklore Around the World, the Bible's Relevance Today, and Advanced Piano Workshop. Classes in singing and folk dance; workshops in theater, writing, and painting; and physical fitness exercise classes are also available.

How the Curriculum Is Established

Most LIRs have a curriculum committee which plays a major role in determining the mix, academic level, and format of the program. In general, these committees are guided by three critical factors: *first,* the stated or implied philosophy of the LIR or the sponsoring college or university; *second,* the process by which members are involved in determining which courses and classes should be included in or excluded from the program; and *third,* the facilities available for carrying out the program.

In curriculum planning, four areas will require a resolution of philosophical differences. *First,* there is the need to establish a sense of the appropriate balance among academic, recreational, leisure-time, and social programs; or, differently stated, the level of intellectual activity desired in the program. *Second,* decide the extent to which the LIR is to be a peer-learning organization—that is, whether the study-group leaders should come solely from the membership, from both the membership and outside resources, or entirely from outside resources (either regular college faculty or other specialists). *Third,* determine whether all study-group leaders or teachers must be experts in the area being studied, or whether the groups also can be led by members who are "first among equals," as in the Great Books Discussion tradition. *Fourth,* assess the minimum amount of outside preparation, if any, that is expected or required for participation in classes or courses. These decisions have significant influence on the mix of courses, the intellectual level of the courses offered, and the members' understanding of what is expected of them in helping to maintain the LIR as a member-driven institution.

The process established by LIRs to determine the subjects of interest to members varies from one program to another. The most common method is for the curriculum committee, having considered the philosophical issues, to make a preliminary screening of course suggestions submitted by the LIR memberships. Questions of program balance, academic level, leadership possibilities, and potential for member involvement are discussed. The list of courses approved by the curriculum committee is then sent to the membership at large, who check and return to the committee those courses that they think should be offered. The final program is established from these returns.

A variation of this model is conducted by "The Plato Society" of the University of California–Los Angeles, where all study-groups are led by members of the program. Special lectures and forums have university faculty or other specialists as speakers. Members are solicited for course suggestions, with or without a recommendation concerning who should lead the group. The curriculum committee screens the suggestions, and the approved list is circulated to the membership. Each member votes for five programs, in order of preference, in which he or she would like to enroll. The committee then looks for leaders for as many of the courses receiving the highest number of votes as space will allow. Once this task has been accomplished, each member will be assigned his or her top two choices, the maximum number each member is permitted to attend.

At Harvard's "Institute for Learning in Retirement," the process begins when members are invited to propose programs which they will lead. All of the Harvard LIR programs are led by members from the program. The proposal includes a synopsis and brief outline of the course, as well as the proposer/leader's qualifications to lead the group. The curriculum committee then reviews the proposal, and if it fits into the framework of total program balance and the proposer is deemed qualified, the course will be included in the next year's curriculum.

The process for establishing the program at The New School's "Institute for Retired Professionals," focuses more on ad hoc planning committees which the curriculum committee sets up for each new course that members suggest and the committee approves. Of the 80 courses offered each year, 60 to 70 are carry-overs from the year before. These include most art, music, and poetry appreciation groups; foreign language classes; and recreational programs and skills workshops. Approximately 12 to 16 courses are new each year. Typically, the committee will approve some 15 to 20 proposed courses, and invite members to serve on an ad hoc planning committee for a course in which they are interested. Members of the planning committee (at least eight members must attend the initial meeting) decide whether the course should be offered, and if so will work with the proposer to develop the course outline and format. When this task is completed, a search will be made for one or two members to lead the program. If one is found, the course will be offered the following year. If no member agrees to lead the program, then the proposal is dropped.

The availability of appropriate space, on- or off-campus, plays a major role in determining the number of programs to be offered, as well as the format for particular programs. Many of the LIRs have had to supplement the space offered by the sponsoring college or university by using a variety of community resources as well as private homes. At "The Plato Society," all study-groups are held in a downtown Los Angeles building owned by UCLA. Classroom size limits all these programs to 18 participants. For their larger activities, especially the symposia, the UCLA LIR rents facilities in a nearby church. At American University's "Institute for Learning in Retirement," which originally had conducted its program within the Washington, DC campus, it was also necessary to move the office and classrooms from the campus to a nearby church.

Other arrangements for class meetings are to be found at the "Five College Learning in Retirement Institute" in western Massachusetts, where classes are held in each of the five sponsoring colleges—Amherst, Hampshire, Mount Holyoke, Smith, and the University of Massachusetts. Perhaps the most widespread class meeting places are those of the two LIRs at California's San Diego State University, Rancho Bernado and San Diego. Classes there meet at the two colleges as well as in a variety of churches, community centers, and private homes throughout north and south San Diego County.

Formats and Levels of Participation

The opportunity to bring to the classroom the ideas, insights, and experiences of the participants provides the essential thrust of most LIR academic programs. Thus, the discussion format is emphasized. Where such other formats as lectures, panels, workshops, or small buzz groups are used, time is generally allowed for participants to exchange views.

No fixed pattern emerges for the number and schedule of sessions for particular courses. The members of each program determine a schedule most convenient for them. Many of the programs follow the academic calendar of their sponsoring institution and run for the most part on a semester basis, meeting once a week. In some other places the schedule is independent of the sponsor, and the courses run through the fall and spring semesters, meeting once every other week. Elsewhere the semester is shortened to six or eight weeks, or perhaps two short series of four- to six-week programs are run each semester. The subject matter of the program often determines the length of the course and the frequency of meetings. Thus, with few exceptions, workshops and foreign language classes run throughout the year and meet weekly; recreational classes meet as the spirit moves the members.

In most LIRs, especially the mid-size to larger ones, a mix of formats for the different class offerings exists. Perhaps typical is the following statement from the catalog of the "Continuing Learning Experience Institute" at California State University at Fullerton:

> "*Meeting Times*—Lecture/Discussion Groups are ordinarily scheduled every other week. Study Groups are scheduled every other week unless some contingency makes weekly meetings more desirable, as in the case of languages. Activity Groups are scheduled to suit the particular activity. The Distinguished Lecture Series meets on specified Thursdays at 1:00 P.M.

The size of classes will depend on both the format being used and the facilities available. Discussion groups typically limit themselves to 20 participants, although in some programs the number of participants in a group will vary from perhaps six to 40. Workshop programs may have a limit of around 14 members, but in larger LIRs the number might range from six to 25. In lecture groups only the size of the facility limits the number who can attend. Several LIRs have lecture programs in which 125 and more members participate. Most of them have a policy of ending the lectures with a serious effort at discussion; some organize small buzz groups or listening teams to give more participants a chance to be heard. At the very least, the lecture sessions will end with questions or comments from a few of the members. Sometimes, unfortunately, there are *too* few to be considered a true exchange of views.

Participants' class preparation varies with the nature of the subject being considered and the philosophy of the program. Because class size is limited, and the facilities or leadership resources do not permit a larger number of classes to be scheduled, some programs limit the number of courses in which members will be permitted to enroll. In other cases, no limit is put on the number of classes a member may attend. In The New School's LIR, where there is no formal enrollment in classes, members may attend as many programs as they wish which do not have specific requirements for attendance. A number of members attend both morning and afternoon programs, four days a week.

In some programs the curricular philosophy requires enrollees in study-groups to be actively involved in the conduct of the group. Such involvement will be either as the leader of one of the sessions, or as a presenter of a research paper which will serve as the background for discussion by the class. Other courses require members to complete assignments in preparation for the next class session if they wish to participate in the study-group. Sometimes it is "expected" rather than "required" that leadership, research, or other assignments will be carried out. In all of the larger programs the mix of activities permits members to attend some classes in which they will do no outside preparations, and others in which they will be fully involved in at least one class.

Finally, all LIRs recognize and accept the fact that such planned or unplanned events as travel, sickness, the need to care for others, or visits from family or friends may interrupt or deter preparation of assignments. Despite this sort of happenstance, continued participation in the group is lovingly encouraged.

Selecting Instructional Leadership

The task of finding and selecting instructional leadership is common to all member-driven programs. Normally assigned to the curriculum committee as a practical matter, the job may be shared by the officers and council members, past and current coordinators of groups, and those who hold leadership roles in the program. It is a continuing assignment for all of them.

The search for and selection of instructional leaders begins with a review of the application for membership; it continues at the first and subsequent meetings for new members; it is carried on in the classrooms by the group leaders; and it is an ongoing interest for officers and council members in their informal lounge discussions, the rap sessions, the brown-bag luncheons, and the cafeteria. It goes on everywhere.

A number of LIRs make effective use of a skills bank which lists the former occupation and present hobbies and skills of all members and is kept up-to-date. The skills bank is used by program leaders and the curriculum committee for finding members who have the abilities needed for leading proposed study-groups. Sometimes members of the admissions committee advise particular study-group leaders that a new member who shows a lot of promise will be joining his or her group. The committee member recommends that, if possible, the study-group leader encourage the new member to become a paper-presenter, or take on some other group leadership role. Also, asking a member who may feel uncertain of his or her ability to become a study-group leader or to serve for a period as a co-leader with one of the experienced leaders may help.

Most of the programs agree on three characteristics they look for in study-group leaders: (1) the ability to work with others to design a curriculum which meets the interests of participants in the group; (2) the skills of persuading members of the group to share in the leadership role—as a presenter of background reports, or as a group librarian or secretary; and (3) the competence to lead discussions after the background presentations have been made. Some sharp differences exist, however, about a fourth quality: the degree to which the leader should be knowledgeable in the subject area of the class.

This fourth quality—the leader as expert—is most keenly felt where all study-group leaders must be members of the program. While there are few differences among the LIRs on the desirability of having leaders who have some degree of professional expertise, almost all will accept for some of their programs members who are not experts in the particular subject area, but who have an enthusiasm about the subject and will serve as the first among equals.

Some subject areas, however, call for special knowledge by the leader. In foreign language classes, and workshop and skills programs, where the participants are interested in acquiring a new skill or learning the specifics of a subject, a content specialist must lead the group. Here, the traditional classroom model exists: student and teacher, one learning from the other. In programs that do not have members qualified to lead these groups, such classes cannot be held. A similar problem exists in most of the math and science areas where the leadership must have an appropriate background in the subject. Few members whose work and education have been in nonscientific fields are able to engage in a discussion about math or science without the guidance of someone knowledgeable in the field. Again, the teacher–learner pattern provides the model.

On the periphery of scientific inquiry, however, interested and enthusiastic amateurs *can* provide leadership. In one study-group on "Uses of the Computer," which proved to be quite successful, neither the group leader nor the participants had any experience in operating a computer. Their careers were as librarians, lawyers, physicians, businessmen, and teachers. The outline for the course required that at each session one of the members of the group would tell how the computer was being used in his or her industry or profession. A program titled "Science Changes the World," in which members of the class (none of whom was trained as a scientist) told how their industry was being changed by new scientific discoveries, was an equal success.

In study-groups in the humanities and liberal arts, however, the need for specialists is not so pressing. In those areas, interested amateurs can lead the programs, with the expertise required for any class coming from the assigned readings, supplemented by the presentation of a background paper prepared by a member of the group. In these instances the leader is neither teacher nor instructor, but more the facilitator who helps draft the course outline, organizes the class sessions, recruits the presenters, and conducts the discussions following the presentations.

When a program uses outside instructional leaders, either regular university faculty or local experts, the task of finding someone to lead study-groups is much easier. In these situations the concern of the curriculum committee is largely limited to having the outside instructor try to involve the members of the group in as much discussion as possible. There are both benefits and liabilities in going outside the LIR membership to find experts to lead classes. One advantage is that programs which might not otherwise be able to be offered can be put into the curriculum. (The disadvantage, from the point of view of those programs that insist on having only members lead groups, is that the outsiders diminish the LIR's objective of demonstrating that older people can take charge of their continued growth through self-help groups which they themselves organize and lead.) A second advantage of going outside the LIR is that it brings to the class members the best expertise available. (The disadvantage, say the peer-learning groups, is that there is far less involvement by participants in groups led by outside experts than there is in groups run by class members.) The best thinking in the humanities and liberal arts may not be expounded by the expert in the class, but rather evidenced in the books read in preparation for the classes, and by the exchange of insights gained through a lifetime of living.

At least three more practical issues arise for programs using outside experts. *First:* Should stipends be given to outsiders, while LIR members who lead groups and also are experts in their fields are not paid? The member–expert understandably may resent this different treatment. The matter remains a constantly delicate issue.

Second: There is difficulty in encouraging members to lead groups if they are not experts in the particular fields to be discussed. Many members who already are diffident about becoming study-group leaders will be even more reluctant if their amateur efforts are measured against the skilled teaching of trained professional lecturers.

Third: It is easier to listen to an expert than to be actively involved in a discussion led by a member who is a first among equals. A kind of academic Gresham's Law may move members to the less taxing group.

A comparison of the benefits and costs of using outside experts in LIR study programs leads to the conclusion that no single correct position prevails. Local conditions, the resources within the membership, and the general philosophy and objectives of the members and leaders will determine who the instructional leaders should be.

Level of Academic Rigor

"Testing" and "evaluation" are unacceptable words in virtually all member-driven programs. Members do not want to be judged, and resist and resent any organized effort at testing. Study-group leaders and presenters of research reports do not want to be publicly evaluated by their peers. While many members, presenters, and group leaders will value private and informal discussions and suggestions for improving their performances, they generally will do so only if the suggestions come from those with long experience as group leaders. Almost without exception these discussions will not take place if they are part of a curriculum committee evaluation project.

Feedback on the level of academic rigor in study-groups, however, is always available to the curriculum committee. Publicly or privately, evaluation goes on all the time. For example, members talk with each other outside of the classroom to exchange views on the success or failure of the group they are in, and the reasons for such success or failure. They make judgments about the curriculum design, the effectiveness of the group leader, and other members of the leadership team. Sooner or later these judgments filter back to the curriculum committee, albeit sometimes (unfortunately) in garbled form.

A second means of silent evaluation also goes on—members vote with their feet. They drop out of classes which do not meet the standards they expect, and flock to those whose reputation for high quality is widely reported. In most programs, too, a "star" system often is established: A group leader becomes known as being particularly effective, and it does not matter what program he or she leads; it will be continuously oversubscribed.

A number of programs have tried subtly to institutionalize an evaluation procedure. One frequently applied method is to have participants fill out an end-of-term evaluation questionnaire. The questions attempt to elicit information on the relative success of the classes and the performance of the group leaders. By and large, the results of the questionnaire have not been very successful. If the result of the evaluation is even slightly negative, no matter how delicately the matter is discussed with the group leader, it is resented. However, the questionnaires on occasion have been *somewhat* useful, in reminding members to be concerned about questions of academic quality.

Because there have been *no* studies by outside investigators of the academic levels attained by study groups in member-driven programs, the following comments come largely from discussions with leaders and directors of LIRs across the country.

Academic levels and the rigor of the study-group programs are highest in the smaller groups wherein participants are required to prepare for all class sessions by doing outside reading, and also to generate a modest paper supplementing the reading for at least one of the sessions. Leaders and directors are in general agreement that the level of presentations and discussions in these classes is comparable to that in first- or second-year graduate programs.

A much lower level of academic rigor exists in discussion groups, frequently dealing with current events, wherein outside readings are left up to the participants. In these groups the level is frequently that of intelligent conversation, rather than a search for deeper understandings or insights.

Often the groups become platforms for members who seek to expound on their pet biases. Between these high and low levels are the lecture programs in peer-learning LIRs, led by a group leader who has recruited members to present research papers which serve as the basis for much of the discussion. The lecture groups can be as small as 20 or as large as 150, and in many of them most of the attendees will not have done *any* preparation for the class. In most instances it is not unusual for the peer lecturer to spend 100 hours "and a lifetime of experience" in preparing for the presentation. The presentation will be first-rate, and the discussion that follows equally good.

There is a "however" here: The level of academic rigor will vary from session to session when the lecture format is used with a different presenter at each class. Sometimes, because of inexperience as both teacher and lecturer, the presenter talks too long, and there is little opportunity for discussion of the subject by the members. At other times the material in the talk is excellent, but the speaker's delivery makes him or her difficult to understand. Too, on occasion the presentation content will not lend itself to discussion.

In general, the quality level of work in the art, writing, poetry, and other workshops is quite high, and compares favorably with that of similar courses offered in university noncredit continuing education classes. The members are uniformly serious about their efforts, and the classroom atmosphere reflects that. In the crafts, hobbies, and exercise classes, as well as the leisure-time bridge, chess, and folk-dance groups, the programs are fully enjoyed but still leave enough energy for members to engage in the more academically rigorous programs.

Maintaining Academic Standards

Although member-driven programs retain control over their academic offerings, the sponsoring universities play an important role in maintaining the standards. This is done mainly through the university's paid staff member assigned to the program. The staff member, usually called the director or executive secretary, typically serves as both the LIR's representative to the university (usually the dean of the school administering the program) and the university's representative to the LIR.

In the latter role, the director works with program leaders in emphasizing and helping to carry out the academic standards which the university expects to be observed by each of its constituent units, including the LIR. At universities which do not assign a staff member to the LIR, the task of monitoring standards, if it is done at all, is left to the dean of the sponsoring unit or one of his or her assistants.

Maintaining academic standards calls for the same set of concerns as called for in the establishing of the program. A commitment to serious academic study must be maintained; the members admitted to the program must have the background to meet the level of serious academic study set by the program and the sponsoring university; members must be aware of the special demands placed on them in a member-driven program; finding and developing qualified group leaders must be done carefully; and the available facilities must lend themselves to a program wherein standards can be maintained.

Most LIRs recognize that the maintenance of academic standards begins with the introduction of new members into the organization. Many of the programs have established a series of events to give these members an accurate picture of the organization they are joining, and the seriousness of its academic program. These might include an open house, whereat prospective members can hear about and see the program in action; an interview with a member of the admissions committee; and orientation meetings for new members. Each event is designed to give the new member an accurate view of how the LIR differs from traditional continuing education classes, of the special needs of self-help education programs, and of the role of nonprofessional teachers; and also a clear perception of the concept of an organization in which all members can be both teacher and student at the same time.

To assist those who have been members for some time and would like to teach or to present research papers in one of the classes, a number of programs now schedule meetings for them with staff of the university library. At these meetings, the staff discuss how the library operates (especially the reference section) and what help the librarians can offer. One program that scheduled a workshop on "How to Present a Background Paper" found *no* members interested in the prospect. They did not want a formal session on how to present their papers! Informal private talks with potential presenters, however, proved to be quite acceptable.

All programs recognize that instructional leadership is a major factor in the maintenance of academic standards. Accordingly, many of the curriculum committees now conduct one-day (or half-day) workshops each semester to upgrade the quality of current and future group leaders. The "Plato Society" goes beyond the short workshops: Their group leaders go away on a weekend retreat to consider the issues involved in conducting classes for older persons.

The thrust in many of the group-leader workshops is an exchange of experiences by the leaders on what does and what does not work in their groups. The topics for the most part cover the bread-and-butter issues of leading a group: dealing with participants who talk too much (or not enough), how to get presenters to shorten their talks, stimulating participants to complete their reading assignments, keeping discussants on the topic, and framing questions. The major concerns in many of the workshops deal with successful efforts at getting greater involvement by participants in the groups, how to get feedback from group members on what the group is doing well or not so well, and what it should be doing differently—if anything.

Auxiliary Educational Programs

Membership in a university-sponsored member-driven LIR opens up a wide variety of other special educational programs which go well beyond the study-groups or classes of the program. These special programs include both academic and enrichment programs as well as opportunities to engage in community service. Not the least of the special programs is the variety of social events that the program sponsors.

One of the more popular educational programs that members typically enjoy is participation in the university noncredit continuing education classes open to members at no cost or at a reduced fee. At The New School's "LIR," program members enroll in over 200 different university-run courses each semester. These classes include sculpture, poetry writing, calligraphy, music, philosophy, history, literature, the humanities, and math and science classes not currently offered by the LIR. The value of these programs (aside from the pleasure, information, and insights they bring the members) is twofold. They make possible study with regular college faculty members, thus supplementing the peer-led programs of the LIR. In so doing, the LIR members are able to get the best of both kinds of education. Also, these classes provide an intergenerational learning situation—one in which the members can share their lifetime experiences with the enthusiasms of the younger students.

In addition to the university classes open to LIR members, most of the sponsoring universities invite LIR participants, as members of the wider university community, to attend special university lectures, art shows, concerts, and performances—usually at student rates! (In some programs, members are able to return the favor and invite the wider university community to attend the poetry readings and concerts given by LIR members as part of their regular program.)

Two of the most popular nonclass activities grow out of art and writing workshops. From their painting, sculpture, ceramic, and photography workshops, several programs sponsor an annual art show whereat members exhibit the results of their creative efforts for colleagues, family, friends, and the rest of the interested total community. A similar project grows out of the writing workshops. Here the poetry, short stories, and essays that members have written (in *and* out of class) are assembled in an annual literary journal distributed to all LIR members, the university family, and community groups.

Many of the LIRs now sponsor outreach and service programs, both inside and outside the university. Within the university, members in several of the programs volunteer their services to the "English as a Second Language" (ESL) program and work on a one-to-one basis with foreign students to help then with their English language skills. Another group of volunteers serve as counselors to undergraduate students. Perhaps the most ambitious program is carried on by several members of the "Academy of Senior Professionals" at

Eckerd College in St. Petersburg, Florida, who serve with regular faculty members as co-instructors in the undergraduate division of the college.

In the wider community, a number of LIRs sponsor programs at senior centers, social agencies serving the elderly, and nursing homes. Members give talks, read poetry, and perform choral and instrumental recitals at these institutions. Members of the Brooklyn College LIR "Theater Workshop" regularly perform, at social service and school groups, scenes of plays rehearsed in the LIR workshop.

Conclusion

It is worth noting that in almost all LIRs, as in the universities that sponsor them, learning is a social as well as an intellectual experience. Serious study can be difficult, but it can be made enjoyable if shared with others whose learning interests provide a foundation for new friendships and a social network as satisfying as that developed with colleagues in the work years. The end-of-term class parties, the rap sessions, the coffee klatches in the lounge, the travel trips, the annual banquets—all create an environment wherein serious learning can be the norm. And fun!

5

Membership: Marketing, Recruitment, and Retention

SARA CRAVEN

Retired adults are, for the most part, very busy adults, but they find time to work into their schedules activities which are mind-expanding. The power and excitement of sharing new ideas with other interesting people in a daily social network cannot be underestimated. The task is to use this understanding in attracting and retaining members.

A group investigating the establishment of a member-driven program for learning in retirement must deal with the issues of membership head-on: What kinds of people would be attracted to such a venture? What would they expect? What are the best ways of reaching them? Only when there is a clear idea of the audience and its needs and expectations can one begin to design and then promote the program—and promotion involves more than just advertising. This chapter looks at the total scope of an LIR program, from curriculum and activities to fees and facilities, in terms of the recruitment and retention of members: It is important to understand what motivates older adults to join LIRs.

Retirement brings with it hopes of time, leisure, and freedom from the constraints of work. Yet many people come to the end of successful careers also wanting to expand their worlds intellectually as well as geographically. They look forward to being able to read without distraction, to pursue a new topic in the library or classroom, and to delve into a neglected area of study. Casual comments heard around the lunch table verify this: "When I was in college I took a lot of business courses. I wish I had taken more literature and history." "I often thought about going back to school but never did it. Now is my chance. I tell my grandchildren that I am going to college, too."

When one thinks of the kinds of people attracted to LIR programs, avid readers are at the top of the list. Whether or not they have extensive formal education, they are curious and well-informed. They remember their school years fondly. LIR members have often taken classes in other adult education programs; they have gone to community lecture series, public forums, and concerts; they have haunted bookstores and watched public television. Their lives have been shaped by ideas and, more importantly, by the active pursuit of *new* ideas. Thinking as an instructor, can one imagine a more exciting group? What more could be asked than a classroom full of well-read, self-motivated, and experienced students?

LIR programs attract not only avid readers, but readers who enjoy the give-and-take of learning in a group. If there were no advantage to the group format, people would stay home and read books, and that would be that. Instead, typical LIR members choose to come together to pursue a common interest. Why? *First,* the instructor has knowledge or expertise, or has access to those who have—either members of the class who agree to undertake specific research projects, or outside lecturers. *Second,* the exchange of ideas during classroom discussion and afterward helps to clarify and elucidate the issues. *Third,* students have the opportunity to get to know each other through the sharing of ideas, points of view, and past experience. It is for these reasons that Chautauqua societies, informal book groups, religious study groups, and the Great Books program have flourished. The excitement of a new idea, shared with others, cannot be underestimated as a primary attraction of learning in retirement programs.

When people retire, the needs that were being met in the workplace need to be met in other situations. While some have considered the psychological and emotional dimensions of retirement as part of their preparation for this phase, many have focused primarily on financial and leisure activities. In the early part of retirement, the process of refocusing and reevaluation occupies a great deal of time and energy. LIR programs often attract those in these first stages, people who are busy sampling the diversity of the community.

Most potential members have been active in civic life—in local politics, charities, and religious organizations. They know that these activities have made a difference in the well-being of the community. However, even though these activities can be continued into retirement they often do not meet the same psychological needs, because their role in the individual's life has shifted from auxiliary to central. What was fulfilling on a secondary level may not be enough as a raison d'être.

Marketing Thinking:
What an LIR Offers Its Members

Not only do LIR administrators think about marketing: They market thinking. Paying attention to older people who look forward to continued learning, one must understand which needs an LIR program can address for a retired person, and what members can contribute to each other in order to effectively market the program. Marketing involves the willingness to exchange something of value (usually time and money) to fulfill a need of equal or greater value.

INTELLECTUAL STIMULATION

The desire to learn something new, coupled with the fear of stagnation, leads many people to classes, whether they are in literature or auto mechanics. Rolland Mays (1989), a Duke University institute member and instructor, speaks of people who

> have reached the time of life when they can back away from the motivations that dominated their working careers, and give themselves over to an endeavor which offers something even more valuable than money or prestige, an opportunity to understand themselves and the world around them more profoundly than perhaps ever before. It is a time for objective self-examination in the midst of a complex, indeed awe-inspiring universe they had little time to think about until now. And the richness of that experience will be determined, to a large extent, by the knowledge they have acquired and the pleasure they have learned to take in the life of the mind.

Jules Willing (1981) quotes a retired person with a different point to make:

> What I came to realize is that I consciously had to look for things to think about. Now, that was a startling idea: I never would have believed it if someone had told me it would happen. There never was a time I didn't have things to think about—earning a living, raising a family, managing the household. Even when I retired, I was busy as hell, and had problems to solve and decisions to make. Once that initial period was over, though, there weren't many new problems coming along, and the decisions were about such things as what I wanted to eat for dinner. I found myself sitting on the porch, staring into space, with my mind a blank, although if you asked me I'd say I was enjoying the peace and quiet and looking at the view.
> I began to realize that without having to earn a living, raise a family, manage a household, I'd actually have to find things to think about; that I'd have to provide my own mental input in order to generate any mental output. What an astonishing revelation that was!

STRUCTURE

It is said that when Senator Sam J. Ervin, of Watergate fame, retired to his hometown of Morganton, North Carolina, someone asked him why he continued to go to the office every day. He supposedly said, "So I have a place to go home from." For people retiring from work outside the home, this change of locus is critical. Women whose work has been centered at home have another problem: Their workplace is invaded by a new worker without a specific job description. Restructuring is a complex task, and LIRs can aid in it. Not only do classes provide a place to go home from, but there are assignments to be read, research to be done, presentations to be prepared. There also are committees to be chaired, meetings to be attended, social functions to be arranged. Some attack these enthusiastically, in some ways replicating their work lives. Others just as enthusiastically stay away from anything reminiscent of the organizational world. A promotional flier for the "Institute for Continued Learning" (ICL) at the University of California–San Diego speaks directly to these issues: "Do you miss, or will you miss, the stimulation of your former activities? The associations? The zest for living inspired by all your contacts with so many interesting people?" An LIR becomes part of the retiree's regular schedule: Tuesdays and Thursdays for classes, Wednesdays for golf or bridge, Fridays for Meals on Wheels.

FRIENDSHIP

The possibility of meeting people with similar interests is a primary attraction of all adult education programs. For retirees, LIRs provide the opportunity to fill some of the gaps created when they left the ready-made camaraderie of the workplace.

The issue of friendship is especially important to people who have chosen to move in retirement, to be near children and grandchildren, to take advantage of recreational attractions and medical facilities, or to enjoy a warmer climate. They are acutely aware of the need to establish lives independent of younger family members, and to become integrated into the larger community. While the curriculum of the LIR attracts many initially, the sense of community and the friendships formed are what keep members returning semester after semester. The program's extracurricular activities—including social events, attendance at theater productions, special-interest groups, outside lectures, and short trips—provide an opportunity for people to get to know each other outside the classroom setting.

Not only newcomers feel the need to establish a new circle of friends. Widowed and divorced adults, even though they may be long-time members of the community, often feel the need to form a circle of friends that is not couple-oriented. And even couples, not used to 24-hour togetherness, often speak of the need to pursue independent activities.

In beginning programs, the camaraderie and sense of purpose among the pioneer members is strong. As these programs grow or mature, one must work harder to maintain the warmth and sense of community that attracted members in the first place. Strong leadership at the board and committee levels fosters the development of friendships by attending to the details of group activities and opportunities for participation.

PURPOSE AND CHALLENGE

Retirement does not imply the abandonment of purpose and challenge. On the contrary, efforts at refocusing and reevaluating only heighten the retiree's awareness of what is important and what is not.

> Those of us who have sought to conduct ourselves with some sense of purpose and self-understanding have been in charge of our own lives and have been in control of the situations which affect us. Are such people a majority of older Americans?
>
> I am not sure. But I know that the members of our centers for retirement are a command generation. At least they have high E.Q.'s (energy quotients). They have chosen us. They have chosen to come to our colleges and universities with a purpose, and that purpose is to stay in charge of their lives *through learning*. Above all, it behooves us to recognize and respect this primary characteristic, let us call it energy, purpose, vitality—*authority*—of the group we are serving. (Stern, 1988)

In a different vein, one LIR member reflects on the philosophical challenges that are addressed by the humanities:

> Our challenges are not at the root economic and political, they are rather moral and spiritual, that is, they arise out of the deepest levels of the human psyche; they challenge our very concept of what it means to be human.
>
> The people of the industrialized world enjoy a remarkably high standard of living in terms of the goods of the earth. But what is happening to industrialized man himself? What is happening to that great articulate species, homo sapiens, that is capable of behavior unworthy of the beasts? The human soul is the battleground on which are pitted the forces of good and evil: love and hate, peace and war, compassion and cruelty, courage and cowardice. It is out of that struggle, ladies and gentlemen, that the great literature, the great art, the great heroes of the ages have emerged. They have earned the right to be heard. (Mays, 1989)

These viewpoints represent only two of the many intellectual challenges awaiting the retired adult. Understanding the nuances and subtleties of these viewpoints, and how they are translated into action, results in recruitment efforts that speak directly to the needs and interests of past and prospective members.

Attracting Members

How does one go about presenting the program to potential members? What resources are available to them? What are some of the marketing pitfalls?

THE HIGHER EDUCATION CONNECTION

The university/college connection cannot be overemphasized as both a source of strength and a marketing device. At the most basic level, various community outreach programs within the university have their own mailing lists. Concert and lecture series, art museums, drama departments, and other continuing education programs may have lists of people with interests similar to those of members of LIRs. Most departments are willing to share their lists, seeing LIRs not as competition but as another way of attracting people to the campus. The alumni office can provide names of local alumni who have graduated in specific years.

The educational and cultural advantages offered by an institution of higher learning are strong drawing cards in the efforts of many communities to attract retirees, and an affiliated LIR provides an entree for the newcomer into the life of the university/college. "The Plato Society," in its descriptive literature, aptly describes its relationship to UCLA as "a partnership between the university and retired professional, executive, and artistic people."

INTERNAL MARKETING

Careful marketing within the university will not only help obtain the administration's continued support; it will also provide the institution with a visible example of its service to the community. The university may choose to highlight the LIR in newspaper articles, alumni magazines, and other media presentations. Contacts with appropriate administrators should be made, and brochures can be distributed to campus libraries, alumni offices, medical departments, university benefits and retirement-plannning programs, and public relations offices. The best way to increase awareness among the college faculty is to invite them to lecture in the LIR. While many of them may be reluctant to commit to a full course of a dozen or so daytime classes, often they are able to provide at least a guest lecture or two. And faculty members can help establish a network of academic connections, often suggesting colleagues who are especially knowledgeable on specific topics. The "Academy of Lifelong Learning" at the University of Delaware conducts a once-a-week noontime enrichment program which is presented by university faculty.

TELLING THE STORY: WORD-OF-MOUTH AND PRINTED MATERIALS

As indicated in Chapter 3, the experience of many established LIRs is that word-of-mouth is the most effective method of recruiting new members. The initial steering committees must necessarily include those people with wide networks of community associations. Their natural enthusiasm and commitment will be a beacon for other retirees interested in academic study. Often this core group will include retired people who have been active in other continuing education programs sponsored by the university: non-credit enrichment classes, course auditing opportunities, tuition-waiver classes, and other special privileges for seniors. After the first semester, or even during it, satisfied participants will begin to tell others. An invitation to a newcomer to visit a class or attend an open house is both a gesture of friendship and evidence of pride in the program.

A good reputation, essential to word-of-mouth publicity, is not the same as image. A good reputation connotes a satisfied consumer, one who has experienced the program and liked it. Image, used effectively in the media, is more superficial, less personal, and perhaps less substantiated in fact; its advantage is that it can be used to spark the interest of a larger number of potential participants.

An open house is another good way to introduce the program to newcomers. In an informal setting, around coffee and cookies or wine and cheese, prospective members can meet current members and coordinators of classes and begin to evaluate the program in terms of their own expectations. It is important to have a brief program as a focus of the event—at least a welcome from the university administration, an instructor/coordinator, or a fellow-member. At Duke University a member has developed a humorous slide presentation, lasting only about five minutes, which covers quickly *all* the important aspects of LIR life. This is the same slide show that staff and board members use when asked to introduce the program to civic and retirement groups.

One step removed from individual recruiting contacts is the "chicken and mashed potatoes" circuit of newcomers clubs, neighborhood groups, book clubs, civic clubs, and religious groups. Members of the LIR steering committee can help make contact with the program chairperson of these organizations and volunteer to make a presentation.

Paying attention to printed materials is critical. The course description brochure, new each semester, need not be lavish but does need to be attractive and well-written, using a large, easy-to-read typeface. In the beginning of a program there may not be many courses, so there probably will be the luxury of adequate space in the brochure for enticing course descriptions. Including a sentence or two about the instructor or coordinator serves to begin building rapport even before the class starts. Well-written and specific course descriptions have a number of subtle functions beyond merely announcing the course: They show that good writing is valued, that the class is well-organized, that the program wants people to know what to expect. Ask instructors to write their own course descriptions, then edit for length and style. (Instructors usually write enthusiastically about the topics they teach!) The descriptions of other activities, from special-interest groups to evenings at the theater, from literary magazines to fiction contests, reflect the varied interests of the members as well as the benefits of being a part of the university community.

A second kind of printed material is the general information brochure, which describes the program in nonspecific terms, without the details of course descriptions and set schedules. It is appropriate for distribution by realtors, chambers of commerce, churches, and other agencies where people go to learn more about the community and where the detailed course brochure might become outdated. Welcome Wagon organizations willingly distribute this kind of material.

Once people can be enticed to pick up and read the printed material, the program will sell itself because the depth and breadth of the curriculum suggest a group of serious participants committed to the joys of inquiry and discussion. Thinking back to the kinds of people who are attracted to LIRs, and for what reasons, we can see that the following suggestions may be helpful for distributing written materials:

- Places where readers go: libraries and bookstores
- Places where people wait: professional offices
- Places where people congregate: neighborhood and apartment centers, restaurants, shopping centers, and churches
- Places where newcomers go: realtors, chambers of commerce, Welcome Wagons, and newcomers clubs
- Cultural events: concerts, theaters, art galleries
- University public relations and continuing education departments
- Personnel departments in industry, and retirement planning consultants in the community
- Community clearinghouses on issues of aging
- Geriatric treatment and research programs, in both the university and the community

Because LIR programs target only a small segment of the community, large-scale bulk mailing blanketing the community would seem to be effective only if there were identified residential or zip-code areas heavily populated by retired people. However, there are many private marketing firms which can target not only retired people, but those with specific educational levels and academic interests. List brokers have access to lists of newcomers, empty-nesters, and travelers. The Elderhostel Institute Network, a consortium of LIR programs, will provide zip-code specific mailing lists of those who participate in standard Elderhostel offerings, i.e., the one-week residential programs.

A small and carefully tended mailing list is an invaluable asset. A member with computer skills might be tapped to maintain the list, keeping careful track of how many mailings have been sent to a particular address and noting the response. Ask current members to give the addresses of potential members.

USING THE MEDIA

Gaining access to the local media can be a time-consuming and frustrating project for an organization. Again, the university connection is invaluable in this regard because the public relations office or news bureau is mandated to promote university projects. Staff members can advise on appropriate media, the format of press releases, and optimal timing. They can suggest editors and reporters who might be especially interested in the program. Often they will write a feature article, highlighting a particular coordinator or course, and distribute it to newspapers in the area. Read the local newspapers carefully to become familiar with the kinds of announcements that appear in various calendars. Send course brochures to editors and reporters who write about education, aging, or a specific class topic such as art history, meteorology, or creative writing.

Local radio and television stations make public service announcements. Call them to find out the correct format. Short announcements, 20 seconds or less, are more likely than longer ones to be aired during daytime and early evening hours. Talk shows, on both radio and TV, also are a good resource, and some LIR members almost invariably can be persuaded to speak on their favorite course topics.

RECRUITING IN RETIREMENT COMMUNITIES

Recruitment among members of retirement homes and communities may seem a natural step, but LIRs do not appear to draw substantial numbers from these settings. (At Duke University, for instance, less than 2 percent of the LIR members live in residential retirement communities.) Many residential homes provide educational and recreational programs on-site, and residents prefer the convenience of not having to drive, park, and then perhaps walk a considerable distance to the classroom. If public transportation is not convenient, or if the transportation services offered by the retirement community are difficult to manage, residents may not want to commit to a weekly class elsewhere.

For LIRs with space problems, holding classes in a retirement home may be an option. A drawback is that communication among members becomes much more difficult when classes are moved away from the central location. Although some retirement communities are not eager to have nonresidents using their facility on a regular basis, the "Academy" at the University of Delaware has had great success with an outreach program offering free mini-courses at retirement centers. Over 120 requests are received each year.

SCHEDULING AND FACILITIES

The issues of time and place, further discussed in other chapters, are mentioned here because of their effect on marketing. Most LIR classes and activities are scheduled during the day. The availability of daytime classroom space on campus, while a problem for administrators, is a signal to retired people that attention is being paid to their needs. Many older people feel more comfortable driving or using public transportation during the daylight hours. When several class periods can be scheduled on one day, sometimes with more than one class meeting at a given hour, people are encouraged to attend more than one course, thus minimizing travel and parking woes. Neighbors with dissimilar interests might car pool, and informal socializing will occur in the car as well as around the coffee pot between classes, and over lunch. Care needs to be taken to make it as easy as possible for people to attend.

Sunbelt communities attract "snowbirds" from colder states during the winter; mountain and lake areas attract Southerners and city dwellers during the summer. In order to accommodate both permanent residents and vacationers, the "Institute of Retired Professionals" at the University of Miami has five terms of six weeks each, offering 12–14 courses each term. (Approximately 75% of the members are year-round Florida residents.) Marketing to these groups involves not only the libraries and media already mentioned, but also tourist information centers, condominium areas, and realtors. Communities that attract retired vacationers for stays of several months or more will be better able to support LIRs because the temporary residents will want to establish some ties in the community and will use the program as yet another recreational opportunity.

The facilities in which the LIR is housed play a critical role in recruitment. If the program is lucky enough to have an attractive campus building or an old house, the immediate impressions will be of a campus setting and of home, both of them impressions worth fostering. The Rochester Institute of Technology was fortunate to secure an unused country club adjacent to the campus. If at all possible classrooms, offices, and social areas should be on the first floor, or accessible by elevator. The issues of facilities, of distances between classrooms, of social areas, and of the parking lot, all are important in that they can determine whether or not people will choose to join, and then to return. Furnishings may be plush or barebones—it doesn't matter to most LIR members. Some programs are fortunate enough to have different rooms for seminars, lectures, and social events; more often rooms are multipurpose and class members may be enlisted to rearrange chairs between classes.

Adequate parking, surely one of the most common issues facing university administrations today, affects LIRs, too. If the university is known to have significant parking problems, then access to nearby parking, even for a modest fee, could be a strong selling-point. When new members are oriented to the campus, parking facilities and regulations should be addressed, and a good map is a must.

Commons areas, for socializing before, between, and after classes, are essential. A coffee pot and hot water for tea and hot chocolate, equally so. Keep in mind that the space will reflect the program in countless subtle ways.

It is often possible to expand public awareness, program opportunities, and space all at once by offering cooperative ventures in conjunction with other university or community programs. At Duke University, studio art classes at the local arts council are offered to LIR members at a reduced fee. Both programs benefit, and the LIR does not have to find the specialized space necessary for such classes.

Some Cautionary Notes About Marketing

Successful marketing consists of having a good product, finding the appropriate audience, and ensuring that the two get together. Paying attention to detail can make all the difference.

UNDERSTANDING THE MARKET

Most programs have strong liberal-arts curricula, a feature which may not appeal to the full range of seniors in the community. For marketing efforts to be cost-effective, they must be directed to affinity groups who have the shared characteristics of other members—that is, they are readers, active in community life, and attracted to the educational and cultural offerings found on a university campus.

HOMOGENEITY OF MEMBERS

A word about relying too heavily on recruitment by word-of-mouth: You may attract members with similar backgrounds and interests, and few differences. Diversity of experience and perspective is a great boon to the learning process, so efforts should be made to publicize the program to students in all ethnic, racial, and economic groups. Most LIRs have overrepresentation from women and underrepresentation from Hispanic and black adults. Most LIRs are also overly middle- and upper-middle class, economically.

DISTRIBUTION OF MATERIALS

Often printed materials—course schedules and general brochures—are prohibitively expensive to produce and mail in large quantities. Most LIR budgets permit selective distribution, as opposed to blanketing the entire community. Again, choose places where readers and those attracted to cultural events will see them. In any location, be sure to ask permission to leave a few copies. Some offices, businesses, and public gathering places have strict policies about outside materials. Be careful not to leave too many copies at a given time; they quickly become messy, and office personnel and custodians will throw them away. It is better to return a week or two later to see if the stock needs replenishing.

DIFFERENCES IN MARKETING LEARNING IN RETIREMENT AND TRADITIONAL CONTINUING EDUCATION PROGRAMS

LIRs focus on a smaller segment of the community than do most other continuing education programs, thus necessitating more specialized distribution and mailing. They capitalize on the benefits of participatory learning, of contributions by the members, and of the sense of community generated. True, friendships and the enjoyment of learning in a cooperative atmosphere are aspects of other programs, but the emphasis on membership is different. Because courses are not priced individually, there is no opportunity for differential pricing to attract students, test the market, or assure attendance in a class on a highly specialized topic.

On the other hand, the fact that people are members, with the opportunity to register for a number of courses for a set fee, means that they will sometimes risk taking a course they might not have paid for separately, just because it occurs on the same day as another class. Creative scheduling can provide a ready-made complement of students for unusual, technical, or advanced courses. Location plays a larger role in LIR programs because of the sense of affiliation with the university program as a whole, and because the issues of transportation and parking are more important to older students than to younger ones. These differences must be highlighted in all LIR communications.

Retention of Members: Thoughts on Member Satisfaction

Vibrant, inclusive, adventurous groups have a spirit that is irresistible. The atmosphere is welcoming and lively, fueled by conversations about issues and ideas. Setting the tone is essential—but *how?* What can institute leaders do to ensure that members feel committed to the program and return semester after semester? What are the group maintenance needs to which attention must be paid?

OWNERSHIP

This cannot be faked. A program run *for* retired people will quickly look like yet another service agency. A program run *by* the members, in collaboration with the university, elicits commitment and enthusiasm that are evident in every aspect of the program. Thus the emphasis in this book on member-driven programs. Given the leadership skills in this group of experienced and well-educated older adults, there should be little difficulty finding people to assume responsibility. Some retired people are admittedly "burned out"; they vow never to go to another committee meeting. (Some even stick to their vows!) But there are others who miss the problem-solving, policy-making, and control they left behind in the business world. The most effective LIR board of directors will reflect the diversity of the membership and will be able to tap its varied strengths. Those who are paid university staff will find it particularly difficult to keep their hands off and allow the program to be run by the members.

ADMISSION CRITERIA

Most programs have open membership. That is, anyone who wants to join is admitted. A smaller number do some screening. The advantage of screening is that it helps to ensure the high standards of participatory learning; the disadvantage is that it may discourage some less self-assured members.

TYPES OF MEMBERSHIP

Members usually join on a semester or annual basis. The Duke University "Institute for Learning in Retirement" has an associate membership, at a reduced fee, entitling people to take just one course. It was introduced at a time when growth was slow and it was thought, correctly, that the associate membership would attract newcomers who would later become full members. LIRs in towns with migratory or seasonal retirement communities need to be creative in providing membership options that meet the needs of both transient and year-round members.

MEMBERSHIP COMMITTEES

The functions of this important committee are varied: hosting open houses, distributing promotional materials, following up with people who do not return, collecting information about members, and compiling demographic data. Committee members representing geographical areas of the city will know the best places to advertise. They will also be able to host informal coffees or potlucks so that members from a given area can get acquainted. If parking and other issues of transportation are a concern, these neighborhood connections can promote carpooling and the inclusion of nondriving members.

Another function of the membership committee is to familiarize newcomers with the campus. A walking tour of the campus, led by a member, not only can point out libraries, eating spots, concert halls, parking areas, and campus transportation, but also can introduce people to the history and goals of the university. Guest speakers—a reference librarian and the university archivist, for example—add variety to the walk and are, in turn, reminded of the existence of this group of older students. Such casual meetings generate firm and useful connections.

GETTING TO KNOW THE MEMBERS

The usual reluctance to wear name tags (or the propensity to leave one's name tag at home) holds true here. Name tags are especially important as the LIR grows and the same students are not in every class. To ensure that as many people as possible will wear them, make sure that the print is large and that the fasteners are easy to use and do not damage clothing. Spending a little extra on name tags, perhaps charging members a nominal fee, pays off. (Hand-crafted name tags provided for a five-dollar donation have brought in over $5,000 for one enterprising LIR.)

Talented photographers are in almost every program. If they are reimbursed for their expenses, they may be cajoled into putting together an album of current members, which is invaluable in matching names and faces. (After having asked someone his or her name several times, and been introduced a time or two more, it is less embarrassing to check the album than to ask again!)

Instructors, especially new ones, often ask students at the first class to introduce themselves and to identify their interest in the subject matter. This helps not only in learning names, but also in understanding the students' points of view.

Informal get-togethers, parties, ice cream socials, and open houses at the LIR as well as in private homes, help promote the esprit de corps that is such an attractive part of program life. Bag lunches, lunchtime foreign-language tables, and the presence of nearby (walking distance) eateries have similar impact. If space permits, a special lunch room can be used to encourage these social encounters.

Duke Institute members have lunchtime privileges in the nearby faculty dining room. Large tables encourage the inclusion of newcomers. The dining room, one of two, is not well-used by faculty, who tend to be teaching on another part of the campus during the middle of the day. Were it not for the patronage of LIR members, the eatery would surely have to close its doors.

A membership information form is used by many programs. It has several functions beyond the obvious one of getting to know members better: It can be used to solicit potential instructors, coordinators, and committee members; to gather suggestions for future activities and classes; and to find out how people learned about the program. A volunteer, usually a member of the membership committee, is assigned the task of making sure that new members are surveyed. If the LIR has an admission screening process, this information is part of that procedure.

UNIVERSITY BENEFITS

University privileges, discussed more fully in the section on attracting members, also serve to help retain members, and add greatly to the sense of being a part of the university community.

INTERNAL COMMUNICATIONS

When a program is small, using centralized space only one or two days a week, communication is easy because everyone passes by the central bulletin board, and word-of-mouth reports reach nearly everyone. But as a program grows, the communication problems multiply rapidly. Some classes meet away from the main building, so some people miss announcements on the bulletin board; newsletters are more difficult to circulate; people don't always have access to the central lounge and coffee pot; and the expenses of mailings increase. A workable solution is the creation of a corps of class assistants, one assigned to each class, to act as aides to the instructors/coordinators, and to make special announcements, hand out flyers, and in general act as loci of information on the group as a whole.

THANK-YOU'S

Nothing creates as much good will as a thank-you. Written notes often are savored and kept by the recipients. In the absence of a paycheck, or a favorable job review, a thank-you serves as recognition of the hours of work contributed in the service of the organization. One program holds an annual thank-you luncheon for the faculty which includes a presentation from a distinguished university dean or faculty member.

RETREATS

The pressures on board and staff of recurring and complicated issues can often be mitigated by day-long or weekend retreats. A different setting, away from the telephone, contributes to perspective and insight often lost because of day-to-day tensions. Another kind of retreat, an academic convention for the whole membership on a given topic perhaps tied to the site, can be held over several days and nights. Large facilities are often sponsored by religious groups, and can be rented at reasonable rates. Retreats are especially effective, maybe even necessary, for groups that have grown so quickly that many members hardly recognize each other, much less know each other in any depth. Time must be set aside for informal socializing and unhurried conversation. Beyond that classes, games, short excursions, lectures, and long walks all are conducive to making interpersonal connections.

TURNOVER

It is to be expected that a modest percentage of people will not be members in every term. They did not retire so that they could be locked into yet another schedule. LIR members travel, welcome new grandchildren, tend to their own elderly parents, garden, play golf, and get sick. Some just want some time away from the classroom. Most programs experience a 20 to 30 percent turnover rate in any given year, although many will re-enroll in a future semester. Therefore, recruiting efforts continue in full force each semester, promoting the program to new members and reminding former members as to why they should return.

WHY PEOPLE LEAVE

There are the obvious reasons: Retired people travel, develop new interests, move away. They also face diminishing hearing, eyesight, and mobility. Continuing commitment to the program may become a burden instead of a joy, in the face of limited energy. Though our consciousness is continually being raised about equal access for the handicapped, implementation continues to be sporadic and slow. In this age group, the incidence of serious illness and death increases dramatically. In some programs, staff members attend as many as 10–15 funerals every semester. The losses are felt, but usually not dealt with, within the LIR context, adding to some of the tensions mentioned above.

When nonreturning members are polled, they often cite reasons of travel or other obligations to explain their absences. Occasionally someone will say that there was nothing in that term's curriculum that he or she found particularly appealing. The best way to make sure that constructive criticism is heard, and that members are not leaving for reasons that can be remedied, is to maintain an attitude of openness and responsiveness.

Conclusion

The issues of membership will determine the vitality and marketability of the program. Institutional support will determine many of the externals, such as space, financing, and administration, once a program is underway. However, it is the continuing and creative attention to the "people details" that will determine whether or not the program meets the educational and social goals of its members. LIRs are established to provide a setting in which the joys of learning and the pursuit of understanding can take place in an association of thoughtful people. Satisfied members are both the means and the end to this goal.

6

Resource Allocation and Fee Setting

DONALD E. COLLINS AND JANE S. EESLEY

LIR members are sensitive to monetary issues and their desire to have control in financial decision-making. More than any other factor, the ability to respond to this sensitivity depends on the host institution and the legislative environment in which it must exist. Financial harmony between the LIR and its host will best be achieved by sharing information, clarifying expectations about cost recovery, and encouraging early participation in the decision-making process.

Because member-driven LIR programs are by nature and design democratic in governing style, program participants are likely to expect a higher level of involvement in financial decision-making than continuing education or college administrators are accustomed to provide. What follows here investigates all aspects of financial administration, from determining institutional expectations through setting the membership fee to ensuring the program's future. Throughout this chapter, emphasis is on the philosophical issues that form financial policy and provide options for financial management which are feasible for various institutional settings.

Institutional Issues

LIR PROGRAMS AND INSTITUTIONAL MISSION

Various philosophical issues influence the financial policies of any LIR program. A core matter is the institutional motives for founding such a program. Is the LIR seen as community service? Good public relations? A legislative mandate? A revolutionary educational system? A long-term fundraising opportunity? An opportunity for intergenerational learning? Although few institutions begin LIR programs with a single motive, generally one goal will be the strongest and will influence financial policies. A community service program, for example, is more likely to have lower fees and a generous scholarship policy or flexible payment plans. A program which is largely seen as an academic innovation is more likely to be viewed, in relation to other elements of the institutional curriculum, to be more expensive and less concerned about community outreach. Program administrators who have a clear notion of the institutional mission in developing the LIR program will be most successful in designing effective financial policies.

FINANCIAL POLICIES AND INSTITUTIONAL CHARACTER

More than any other factors, the financial policies and control of the LIR program are determined by the nature of the host institution. While program administrators generally can be flexible in other areas, such as governing structure or curricular development, financial matters often must be administered by strict institutional or legislative guidelines. These guidelines affect how the funds are administered (including accounting practices and budgetary approval), how the fees are set, and whether the LIR program is held responsible for balancing revenue and expenses.

Institutional policy also affects the way the program's budget is developed. Program administrators need to know the answers to the following questions: Will the LIR budget be charged for all administrative time? Secretarial support? Classroom and administrative space usage? Maintenance costs or fees? Utilities? Will there be an institutionally determined fee charged the program for "overhead" or indirect costs? Even the most effective administrator will be hard-pressed to bring an LIR program to financial self-sufficiency quickly if his or her budget is charged for all of these "costs" from the outset of the program.

WHO CONTROLS THE MONEY?

The issue of fiscal control is important—and often controversial. University staff who wish to share financial control with LIR participants may be severely limited due to institutional financial regulations. Public institutions are likely to be quite insistent that public funds be allocated and disbursed by paid institutional staff members as opposed to volunteer LIR members. On the other hand, these same institutions probably receive pressure that public funds be spent in accord with public wishes. The end result often is a very active LIR financial advisory committee or treasurer who understand(s) that, technically, it is permissible to advise, but not make final decisions, on financial matters.

"The Plato Society" at UCLA has a remarkably democratic arrangement with the university. UCLA allows the LIR to keep any unspent revenue, with the caveat that the LIR also is entirely responsible for any deficit. UCLA informs the LIR executive committee what the required personnel costs, rental, and institutional "overhead" will be; and the executive committee then works out its own budget, including setting its own membership fee.

Private institutions show a broad range of fiscal control, from allowing an LIR finance committee or participant–treasurer to make line-item allocations, to permitting only paid staff to participate in financial decision-making. Harvard and Duke Universities, for example, do not include a treasurer among council officers, and have no finance committee. The University of Delaware gives the LIR treasurer full access to university budget data and printouts.

START-UP COSTS

In many cases, LIR programs are based in a self-supporting continuing education division whose revenues can in some way offset the start-up funds or first-year deficits of an LIR program. In such cases, a supportive dean or provost may be willing to ignore the LIR financial deficits as long as other continuing education programs are profitable. Occasionally, continuing education allocates a specific start-up grant; for example, "The Plato Society" received a four-year decreasing grant from UCLA Extension's Research and Development funds. In the case of public institutions, the start-up costs of programs whose tuition and fees are kept low by legislative mandate are generally subsidized heavily by the institution. They may have money earmarked within the state's general appropriation to the university, or a separate appropriation outside the general budget, specifically for the retirement program. Programs legislated but not funded will have to scramble for support from within their fiscal unit or from the chief academic officer.

Institutions may also seek corporate and other financial support to cover start-up costs. Although many programs are allowed to begin on the generally low budget provided by the continuing education unit, some quickly and successfully seek instead, or additionally, corporate and foundation support for start-up costs. Duke's LIR received a three-year, $96,000 grant from the Edna McConnell Clark Foundation for start-up funds. By the end of the three-year period, the Duke program was staffed by a half-time director and was very close to financial self-sufficiency. Such funding eases financial pressure during the initial growth period, and also provides publicity. Most programs take about three or four years to become self-supporting.

POLICIES FOR PROCESSING MEMBERSHIP FEES OR TUITION

In almost all cases, each LIR program develops its own policies for tuition or membership rates, financial aid, and refunds. LIR programs generally are too small to motivate the institution's registrar and financial aid office to develop new computer software for financial management, and most LIR program administrators prefer to have these policies under their own control. LIR programs are likely to process scholarships and refunds much more quickly than their extradepartmental counterparts; the processes are less formal and require a lower level of approval. This internal processing allows greater flexibility to handle issues on a case-by-case basis, and also generates good will when problems are solved quickly. LIR members who may be put off by institutional bureaucracy generally prefer to have their finances managed intradepartmentally as much as possible. As was mentioned earlier in this book, older adults need to feel in control of their situation.

INSTITUTIONAL BUDGETARY EXPECTATIONS AND SUPPORT

Institutional expectations vary with both the host institution and the longevity of the program. The institution's president and/or trustees may expect the program to be subsidized indefinitely, either to cover all direct costs except staffing, or to cover *all* direct and indirect costs, or to cover all costs *and* produce a "return" to the institution's general budget. Duke's "Institute for Learning in Retirement" is charged an annual assessment which is set by the Office of Continuing Education, and Harvard's and Northwestern University's LIR programs are required to return any unspent revenue to the overall budget of the continuing education division. Generally, new programs are subsidized (by providing either a start-up budget, or staff and office support at no charge to the program budget) for the first few years.

Although many public institutions expect to subsidize these programs indefinitely, few private institutions plan to do so. Programs which are from three to seven years old generally can cover all office costs, and at least a reasonable portion of staff costs. In general only the oldest, best-established programs generate enough revenue to cover all their expenses and return money to the institution. These are programs with either a very sophisticated volunteer corps, large memberships, or (more likely) a higher membership fee than average. This higher fee, though, may exclude lower-income participants, or require substantial scholarship funds.

It is helpful to consider a few actual budgetary models. Harvard University staff have described the university's budgetary policy as "Every tub on its own bottom," which suggests that each program must pay for the university services it uses. Harvard's "Institute for Learning in Retirement" must pay for all staff time (which includes a full-time director), fringe benefits, and rental of administrative space as well as two classrooms. Space rentals in the past have amounted to 35–40 percent of the LIR budget. The "Learning in Retirement Association" (LIRA) at the University of Lowell in Massachusetts is a low-fee ($75/year) program which is seen by the institution to be a community service. It is staffed by a full-time university professional who spends two days a week directing the LIRA program. Because his time is "donated" and they are not charged for space rental, the program's budget is quite low. Budgetary matters are handled entirely by continuing education staff, and the continuing education office is flexible about the program's time frame for self-sufficiency.

As mentioned earlier, program administrators need to gauge the level of support that the institution is willing to provide without charge. Few LIR programs actually hire a part- or full-time director at the beginning (except those with generous start-up funds); generally they are developed by existing staff loaned to the program by a supportive dean. Secretarial support also is often provided in this way.

In addition to providing staff time, the institution may allow some benefits or privileges without charge or at a reduced fee. Such may include library privileges, parking, reduced fees for athletic and cultural events, and access to computer and athletic facilities. Some membership-based programs include one free continuing education credit course per term. These "free" benefits make the program much more attractive to participants, and increase their sense of being a part of the campus community.

RELATIONSHIP TO FISCAL GOALS OF CONTINUING EDUCATION

LIR programs may be in a public service department (as Pima County Community College's "Senior Education Program" in Tucson, Arizona, initially was) or report directly to the institution's president (as the "Academy of Senior Professionals" at Eckerd College [ASPEC] does), but most LIR programs are housed in the institution's continuing education unit. Although continuing education divisions may initiate LIR programs with an expectation of revenue returned to the unit in the near future, most find within their early years little likelihood that such self-sufficiency will actually develop quickly. Even when a program has received significant seed money the maintenance of a program requires, as a general minimum, a half-time coordinator, secretarial support, and office expenses.

Let us assume a $30,000 budget, with $15,000 for a half-time coordinator, $5,000 for "a portion of a secretary," and $10,000 for all other office costs. For such a budget, self-sufficiency at $75/year membership fee would require 400 memberships; a $200/year membership fee would require 150 memberships. It is an unusual program that grows to such numbers within the first three years. Even this $30,000 "self-sufficient" budget does not include space rental and overhead costs, which may be formidable. Too as the program grows, increased membership benefits may be desirable (and may be expected): a literary magazine, additional secretarial and administrative support, sponsored field trips, occasional paid speakers—all of which will need to come out of the budget.

Once a program reaches its expected "self-sufficiency," the dean of continuing education and other institutional administrators may wish to start charging for certain other costs: building maintenance, library and computer usage, institutional overhead. Thus the financial expectations of the sponsoring department may shift as the program begins to generate significant revenue. The host unit that provided seed money may expect a now self-supporting LIR program to take its turn in providing seed money for other new programs. Few college divisions are so profitable that they can sustain heavy subsidy of LIR programs indefinitely.

Although it rarely is a primary reason, long-term donor cultivation may be a motive underlying the LIR's founding—which may serve to lower institutional short-term expectations. As many directors of established LIRs have noted, LIR members often develop ties to the LIR's host institution which are stronger than their affiliation with their alma mater of forty years ago. LIRs have generated an impressive number of generous bequests, and deferred-giving programs have been established by institutional development offices to meet LIR member needs. Although such a discussion may sound crass to denizens of the public sphere, private institutions, especially small colleges, may entertain such considerations simply as a matter of survival.

Tuition and Membership Fee Structures

TYPICAL DUES

Membership fees may run from an average of $28/class for Pima County Community College's "Senior Education Program" to the "Academy of Senior Professionals" at Eckerd College (ASPEC), which charges a one-time $1,000 initiation fee plus $50/month maintenance fee, which is paid in four quarterly installments. ASPEC members who live in Florida for just the winter may pay a $150 nonresident-member yearly fee. Duke's LIR offers full membership at $95/semester, or an associate membership at $55/semester (which permits the member to participate in only one study group per term). Harvard's LIR charges $170/semester, which cost includes a library card and one free Harvard Extension course (which would itself generally cost more than $170). Established LIR programs at private universities tend to charge $200–$350/year. The lowest-fee programs will be tuition-based and generally cover course registration only (with no "membership benefits"). The moderate programs will include library privileges, reduced fees for parking, some free social events, and small administrative staffs. The most expensive programs are likely to be older and better staffed, and to include a broader array of related programs and institutional privileges. Some membership-fee–based programs offer discounts for married couples.

TUITION VS. MEMBERSHIP FEES

Almost all LIR program administrators advocate a yearly or semi-yearly membership fee instead of per-course tuition. Legislatures frequently set ceiling prices for senior-citizen per-course tuition, such as those of New York, New Hampshire, and Massachusetts, which require that per-course tuition for seniors at public institutions be either waived (except for a nominal registration fee) or limited to an extremely low charge (such as $25). These parameters effectively make tuition-based member-driven programs financially impossible. Membership-fee programs then become a necessity to ensure that a quality program is administered within the limits of the law.

The benefits of membership fees are as follows:

- Increases the sense of a comprehensive program
- Increases sense of participant ownership of program
- Decreases office expense of tracking registrations/refunds
- Encourages participant involvement, because participating in more than one study group incurs no additional cost

The benefits of per-course tuition are as follows:

- Carries a lower participation cost for those who wish to take only one course
- Encourages participation from those who may be away on a seasonal basis and don't want to pay annual fees
- May be more egalitarian—you pay only for what you receive

ANNUAL VS. TERM PRICING

Annual memberships reduce paperwork, encourage a once-yearly promotional campaign, and provide a more stable program budget. Term pricing encourages participation by people who are away for long periods of time, provides two periods of membership recruitment, and may seem less financially intimidating to first-time participants. Some programs must charge annual memberships in order to retain a stable financial base, even as they recognize that such high initial costs may scare off prospective participants. In response to participant request, most programs now allow term or half-year pricing, even though it is less cost-effective.

ADDITIONAL CHARGES

Campuses without parking constraints are able to offer free parking to program participants, but most cramped campuses are forced to charge for parking privileges for LIR participants. Individual study groups or classes which make extensive use of photocopied materials are likely to charge a materials fee, either levied as a flat fee per term or on a per-page basis. To keep costs down, programs generally take up collections for those benefits or services used by only some of the members. Funds for lounge refreshments generally are donated by individual members directly, or channeled through a social or lounge committee, which takes responsibility for raising the money. LIR field trips will include a fee for actual cost only. Parking stickers are provided at cost rather than subsidized (which would penalize people who walk or take public transportation—practices which institutional administrators are likely to encourage).

DETERMINATION OF DUES

Although most host institutions intend LIR programs to be managed on a democratic basis, the line is usually drawn at the membership fee, which is almost always negotiated between the LIR program director and the dean of the sponsoring academic unit. Determining an initial price can be quite a challenge. Actual direct costs are difficult to project, and the degree of institutional support may be unclear at the beginning of a program. Administrators planning a start-up budget must combine knowledge of their own institution with information from the experiences of other programs. Institutional factors in fee setting would include both initial expectations for revenue, and the cost of programs which could be considered similar—due either to teaching style or to targeted age group.

Although the location and market are factors in fee setting, they generally are considered secondary to the institution's expectation of actual costs. Colleges and universities with strong academic reputations, particularly beautiful campuses, or varied and attractive resources may select a slightly higher fee due to these factors. Conversely, in an area with more than one peer-learning program, keeping the fee low may be a significant incentive for recruitment of new members. Institutions may intentionally select a low membership fee so as to encourage participation of low-income community residents. Once set, though, this low fee may be difficult to raise, and also may seem *too* low for participants who clearly would be willing to pay more for the program. Administrators and participants then will need to decide whether to keep the fee low with subsidies, or to raise the fee and find a way to offer scholarships or flexible payment plans.

It is worth emphasizing that it is very difficult to raise fees once set. Programs would be well-served to start at a higher fee base and be less conservative about the price. Even though they differ in educational philosophy, LIR programs may find themselves competing with evening adult education at high schools and community colleges, daytime noncredit programs, offerings at senior centers, museum education programs, and free-tuition programs at public institutions. Administrators of moderate to high-cost programs will need to be clear in their understanding of budgets and of the benefits of their programs during the time when membership fees are set, because comparisons to these other programs will almost certainly be raised by participants.

Dissension concerning the fee, which has been experienced by programs across the country, may be decreased by an emphasis on the benefits of the college campus and environment. Benefits such as library and computer privileges, and access to athletic and cultural events, may cost the program nothing and even make it seem "worth more." Involving participants with the budget, to the extent that the institution allows, may also decrease anxiety about the fees.

REFUNDS

Most LIR programs have a refund policy but actually grant refunds infrequently. Refund policy generally is determined by the paid staff, in consultation with the LIR advisory committee. Some programs are quite liberal in their refund policy, with the expectation that such flexibility is good public relations. For most membership-based programs, refunds are available only in unusual cases, such as sudden illness, death, or the cancellation of a desired study group.

Staff, Faculty, and Volunteers

ADMINISTRATIVE STAFFING

Every institutionally affiliated LIR program will have at least one paid staff person to serve as liaison, although the degree of administrative support provided may vary widely. Administrators will need to consider the level and amount of paid staff support appropriate both to the institutional mission and to the type of program planned. For example, a tuition-based (as opposed to membership-based) program which features primarily faculty lectures can generally be managed indefinitely by a continuing education administrator already responsible for noncredit programming. The more a program is seen as a total membership program, the more staffing is required to oversee the development of such a community. Institutional traditions, too, will be a factor: Institutions that wish to maintain a high degree of control over such a program will need to provide a higher level of administrative staffing. The benefits of paid professional staff include greater institutional control, increased continuity for the members, and an overall more rapid development because the oversight function is handled more efficiently. The potential problems include a significant drain on the budget, authoritarian staff hindering membership direction of the program, overzealous staff handling tasks that members could take care of just as effectively, and the development of a "we–they" syndrome.

PAID VS. VOLUNTEER FACULTY

The debate over paid versus volunteer LIR coordinators is both financial and philosophical. Peer-learning partisans such as "The Plato Society" and the "Institute for Retired Professionals" at The New School for Social Research discourage the use of paid faculty because they feel it detracts from the educational experience and reduces volunteerism. Northwestern's LIR is entirely volunteer, due both to philosophical preference and the presence on campus of an excellent low-cost daytime lecture series administered by the university's alumni.

Duke's LIR features a variety of faculty arrangements: 45 percent of the groups are peer-led; 45 percent are taught by paid faculty, graduate students, and community experts; and 10 percent are led by nonmember volunteers. Hybrid peer- and faculty-taught programs generally work quite well, although they may occasionally find resentment among volunteer faculty who spend as much time in preparation as do the paid faculty. Pima County Community College's "Senior Education Program" prefers a model of paying all faculty a minimal fee, because hiring faculty affords greater quality control. Although including paid faculty will increase costs, programs which do so are less likely to elicit resistance over membership fees, because faculty salaries are seen as an acceptable expense.

VOLUNTEER SUPPORT

Almost all programs rely on participant volunteers to accomplish some administrative tasks. At the least, programs will have volunteer officers from among the participants; at the most, programs will have an entirely volunteer staff (although this is rare). Volunteers can be a tremendous resource in writing bylaws, preparing mailings, designing public relations plans, producing a newsletter, and completing basic office tasks. Serving as a volunteer provides invaluable support to the program, strengthens the individual's sense of connection to it, provides the opportunity to get to know other program participants (and staff), and deepens understanding of administrative procedures. Although they may initially balk at the idea of volunteering for a program with a membership fee, volunteers come away from the experience with much greater loyalty. True, coordination of volunteers can be a demanding task, because volunteers may not be available exactly when one needs them. Over all, though, involving volunteers is a gratifying and useful undertaking, and a significant cost advantage.

Many programs have found members questioning whether peer volunteer coordinators of study groups should pay the membership fee during the terms in which they coordinate programs. Generally the question is resolved in the affirmative: Coordinators should pay dues along with everyone else. The undergirding philosophy is that coordinating is both a privilege and an opportunity for greater learning. Also, volunteering regularly or serving on the governing board may be as time-consuming as coordinating a study group, so where would the lines be drawn? Low- and moderate-fee programs may simply be unable to forgo that much revenue. Those programs that release peer coordinators from dues argue that it is a way of showing appreciation for service to the program. Such a policy also facilitates recruiting coordinators new to the program.

Developing and Managing the Budget

DECISION AUTHORITY AND RECORD-KEEPING

Due to institutional regulations, final decisions about allocation of funds almost always fall to paid institutional staff, although an LIR advisory committee may be consulted on major decisions. Given these constraints, the role of the LIR's volunteer treasurer may be unclear. Treasurers may report on the financial health of the program, giving an overall picture of revenues and expenses, but few learn the institutional budgeting procedures well enough to interpret budgets fully. For this reason, some programs keep two separate sets of books: one which the institution's budget department provides, and a simplified set kept by the program to depict revenue and expenses in a way that makes sense to the program officers. In almost all institutions, financial accounting is handled through institutional systems; that is, monthly budget reports are provided by the institution. Although programs may choose to keep their own books as well, no program has relied solely on its own bookkeeping.

ROLE OF ADVISORY COMMITTEE OR TREASURER

In low-fee, community service programs the budget may be so small that members feel little need for input in budget allocation. In higher-priced programs, though, financial control may become the ground for political struggle. Programs housed in institutions experiencing "town–gown" hostility may find themselves the target of a variety of unrelated grievances. Participants may want to understand how the money is spent and what the actual costs are—figures which may be difficult to determine when the LIR program's start-up costs are subsidized indirectly by the administrative unit in which the program is housed. Because participants are likely to assume (incorrectly) that faculty salaries are almost the sole cost for a college or university, programs that run without faculty may appear to be cost-free. Jeremy Rusk, founder of the Harvard "Institute for Learning" in Retirement, has described the philosophy of peer teaching as "intellectual bartering." Such a description, though, was never intended to imply that such bartering did not require a significant amount of administrative cost. LIR members who expect the most services from the LIR office may be the same people who balk at the administrative charges that attend the program.

ASSESSING ACTUAL COSTS

Administrators trying to develop a preliminary budget will, as we have already discovered, first need to determine which charges will be levied against the LIR budget from the beginning, and which can be subsidized or absorbed by the parent administrative unit. At minimum, beginning programs will generally be charged for postage, photocopying, and publicity (brochures, advertisements, open houses). If the program is charged for "overhead" at the outset, that figure will probably be determined by the institution's central administration or, in the case of public institutions, by legislative committees. Personnel costs, in all likelihood, will be beyond the administrator's control. Appendix VI shows a typical start-up budget.

STANDARD COSTS

Standard costs will include staffing (administrative and faculty), space rentals, office expense, and indirect or overhead costs. The administrator's salary and benefits will be almost always the largest item in an LIR program budget. Staffing costs vary widely by institution. Although new programs may be developed by "borrowed" staff, most member-driven programs of ten or more years' standing will have at least a full-time director and a half-time secretary. The intermediary staffing arrangements will depend upon staff availability and the financial growth of the program. Secretarial support is likely to be "borrowed" also, as long as is possible. Most new programs need secretarial support sporadically, and these tasks may be added to those of secretaries already accustomed to cyclical patterns in their work. LIR programs with paid faculty will need to determine an appropriate salary for faculty and then add this charge into the budget. Generally this payment is quite low ($100–$300 per term), but administrators have had little difficulty recruiting faculty for such dedicated and enthusiastic "students."

Programs which must pay for rental of classroom and administrative space are likely to find rentals another significant line item within the budget, although some programs have had success with low rental charges from nearby churches and synagogues. Office costs will include telephone, photocopying, postage, brochures/course description materials, rental of audio-visual equipment, and special events. Because the program may rely heavily on photocopied materials for its study groups or courses and because program participants live off-campus, costs for postage and photocopying are likely to be much higher than might be initially expected. Paper and photocopying costs would include the production of syllabi, course materials, bibliographies, course descriptions, newsletters, and materials for committee work. Programs that maintain a sizable mailing list may be shocked by the postage costs of mailing course descriptions, newsletters, and other notices.

Costs likely to be overlooked or underestimated would include (where applicable) rental of meeting space, and building maintenance fees; and it is easy to underestimate too the amount of staff time required to run the program. And subsidized social events (such as open houses, appreciation events, and annual meetings) can become quite expensive as program membership grows.

Related Financial Issues

SCHOLARSHIPS AND FINANCIAL AID

LIR programs offer financial support for tuition or membership fees in a variety of ways. Many LIR programs provide scholarships funded by member donations to a designated scholarship fund. Two other options are (1) to lower the price, or (2) to waive the fee, for people who cannot afford the program—rather than actually transferring money from one account to another. Most scholarships are granted simply on participant request; no documentation, such as tax returns, is required. This flexibility is made easier especially when scholarship funds are donated by LIR members happy to have their money serve such a good cause and disinclined to create elaborate systems for determining financial need. It is common for programs with minimal scholarship funding to provide support only to people who have joined in the past at full price (thus demonstrating their commitment to the program).

Scholarship funds generally are administered by institutional staff, although LIR programs may have a designated scholarship committee. Many programs provide the option for the membership fee to be paid over time; others provide for credit-card payment.

DEVELOPMENT OPPORTUNITIES

Host institutions benefit from member-initiated gifts (both unrestricted and restricted), and some institutions now have designed development campaigns targeted at LIR members, either for endowment funds for an LIR program, or for the general budget of the institution.

Many programs have been surprised by how quickly LIR participants develop an attachment to the host institution. They buy notebooks and sweatshirts from the college bookstore, and consider themselves—appropriately—members of the academic community. Unlike most undergraduates, though, these "students" are likely to have significant financial resources, and their generosity to the host institutions has been impressive. Jeremy Rusk, founder of Harvard's LIR, has pointed out that LIR members on average spend more years on campus than "traditional" students, and thus may form a much deeper attachment.

On the small scale, LIR members may make rather modest annual donations or contributions to their program in honor, for example, of the birthday of a fellow program participant. A group at the "Senior Learning Program" in Tucson which used a video cassette recorder at each meeting took up a collection at one class session and donated a VCR to the program. At Northwestern University, the family of a deceased LIR member designated the program as beneficiary of all honorary contributions by friends and family, which produced over $1,400 in donations. On the grand scale, Harvard LIR members initiated a $1 million endowment for the program, which reached over $250,000 in two years' time. And the University of Delaware's "Academy of Lifelong Learning" has raised $2 million for a new building through its membership. They also sell book bags, and hold clothesline art auctions of members' works, in order to raise special gift funds.

Development offices familiar with their institutions' LIR activities have designed giving programs targeted to LIR members. Universities must be careful, though, not to generate resentment among LIR participants from over solicitation.

LIR staff have occasionally sought money from private and corporate foundations. These benefactors have at times been quite generous—especially with start-up funds (as was Duke's experience), which as a rule are easier to secure than is money for program maintenance or building-funds drives. Some larger foundations have plenty of money targeted for educational innovation, but in general LIR programs seeking foundation support will be most successful zeroing in on smaller, more local foundations.

LAST WORDS ON SELF-SUFFICIENCY

We would advise that each LIR program, to the extent that it is possible, work toward a goal of financial self-sufficiency. Programs that can cover their own expenses gain instant respectability within a college or university, especially in the private sphere. This also ensures that the LIR program does not become a competitor for increasingly scarce college/university core funding. Such stability ensures the future of the program (thus the impetus for the Harvard endowment campaign). It also puts program staff in a better position for making requests and bargaining with the central administration.

One coordinator of a "community service" LIR program admitted that without a stronger financial base, he and his program members felt little freedom to make financial requests of the institution. He compared their status to that of "squatters." Although his chosen word may have been facetious, the experience he described is familiar to many subsidized LIR programs. Lack of financial stability increases the perceived vulnerability of the program, even if institutional administrators express no serious budgetary expectations thereof. Reaching financial self-sufficiency also spares program staff and volunteers alike from continually seeking external support.

Conclusion

When considering the development of an LIR program, administrators should review carefully both their own goals for the program and the traditions of their institution. Institutional requirements and expectations will have a pervasive effect on the program's budget and financial management, from the setting of the initial fee to determining whether an advisory committee should include a treasurer. Initial institutional support must be determined when planning the budget and developing a fee structure. Although administrators may begin an LIR program because it is "a good idea," the program's long-term feasibility will be dependent upon careful financial planning and management, which can ensure an LIR program's future. Clearly, LIR programs must work toward financial self-sufficiency to secure their own future.

7

The Intellectually Restless: View from the Members

HENRY T. LIPMAN

Recreation, art, travel, volunteer work, hobbies—while useful—do not give older adults adequate intellectual and social gratification. They need to know they still have substantial gray matter. Member-driven LIRs accommodate the need for intellectual growth, social interaction, and personal fulfillment in their third age.

In recent years the dramatic growth in the number of colleges and universities sponsoring member-driven LIRs, and the concurrent increase in the number of LIR participants, have given evidence that this new instructional mode plays an important part in enabling at least some older persons to find a partial solution to the problem of "successful retirement." Such retirement means the ability to function independently; to deal realistically with changes in personal health, with family rearrangements, and with friendship losses; and to adapt to a life structure and routine which will provide at least a minimum of satisfaction. It also means the ability to come to terms with the "new" self—to learn to enjoy new events and ideas while letting the "new" self ease into becoming a useful member of a more mature community.

Unfortunately, while the LIR programs do help many members to achieve some minimum level of successful retirement, they do not meet the needs of many other older persons. LIRs are for the most part designed for the relatively well-educated. Older persons with less education are not always comfortable in an LIR. At the other end, since LIRs are not geared to replace graduate study, those wanting advanced academic study do not find the LIR programs relevant to their needs. In addition, there are many well-educated older persons who are not satisfied with the whole concept of peer-learning; they want to study only with regular faculty members.

It is also true that some retirees and older persons cannot find "successful retirement" in the relative quiet of academic study. For example, the workaholic executive may feel that he or she can find satisfaction only in active participation in the world of employment. For others, only total involvement in leisure-time activities, from travel to golf, provides the essential ingredients for successful retirement. Some find satisfaction in craft work, while many find it as volunteers in community or social agencies. Still others find that being involved in political and/or social action programs is what they want to do. Many more who are interested in keeping intellectually alive find satisfaction in community or college adult education classes, without the need to affiliate with an LIR. However, for the increasing number of retirees and older persons who are members of LIRs, the programs do meet many of their needs for successful retirement—and this chapter deals with why LIR members feel so affirmatively about the affiliation.

Every member-driven LIR has a collection of quotations from its members telling how much the program has meant to them. From the "Academy of Lifelong Learning" at the University of Delaware comes the exuberant "The Academy fills my life with music, poetry and drama" from one member, and "The Academy has saved my life," from another. Across the country at the "Center for Learning in Retirement," at the San Francisco Extension Center of the University of California—Berkeley, a member says: "Life grew stale in retirement. Now I'm back in the mainstream, challenged and invigorated."

At the Duke "Institute for Learning in Retirement" (DILR) in Durham, North Carolina, a member writes: "Being involved in DILR has influenced my self discipline, too, because it makes me read things I normally wouldn't. It gets me involved in new ideas, and keeps my curiosity in life aroused. Also, I've enjoyed the social aspect—the warm friendships." From the "Institute for Retired Professionals" at the University of Miami, Florida, comes: "What is wonderful about this opportunity to study is that I can appreciate the subjects much more now than I could 50 years ago when I was a 19-year-old student."

The themes repeat themselves countrywide: intellectual excitement, new friendships, a fresh sense of vibrancy and life, the taking control of life, and new areas for personal growth.

Psycho-Social Needs of Members

The near unanimity of these affirmative responses, matched by a 75 to 85 percent annual reenrollment rate enjoyed by almost all LIRs, makes it clear that LIR programs are helping to meet some of the basic psycho-social needs of members. These needs, shared by older persons generally, are similar to those of other age groups, but manifest themselves in different ways. As Abraham H. Maslow (1970) and others have pointed out, all physically and mentally healthy persons have an interrelated hierarchy of needs. These include: physiological needs (e.g., food, clothing, shelter); safety needs (e.g., security, structure and order, income stability, freedom from fear); belonging and love needs (e.g., affectionate relations with people in one's group, the importance of give-and-take with work colleagues, overcoming feelings of aloneness); esteem needs (e.g., confidence in self and high self-evaluation, receiving praise and respect from others); and self-actualization needs (e.g., to grow to the full extent of one's capacities).

A sharp distinction should however be drawn between these lifelong needs, which are shared by all age groups, and the unique emotional problems that arise from such age-related life crises as a death in the family, illness and pain, sensory loss, and depression. Without gratifying these lifelong needs, Maslow says, people will develop some degree of discontent and restlessness, boredom, loss of zest in life, self-dislike, steady deterioration of intellectual life, and other pathologies.

Some measure of how LIRs help members to satisfy these needs can be gained by looking at what motivated them to apply for membership in the first place. For our purposes, this can best be done by combining Dr. Mark Blazey's study of members, programs, and administration of member-driven programs, reported in Appendix III, with some anecdotal data collected by this author during several hundred interviews with LIR members, program directors, and LIR leadership. Blazey's study points out that LIR members tend to be well-educated; worked as professionals or business executives, or held senior volunteer assignments in community and school organizations; and are in reasonably good health.

There is general agreement by program directors, officers, and board members that most of those who become members of LIRs do not join because they are lonesome and have nothing to do. Their affiliation is not a search for companionship and a place to wile away the hours in pleasant company. As a matter of fact, most members have friends outside of the LIR, and also see their own families quite regularly. Too, many of them, both before they joined and after they became members, remained involved in volunteer activities, hobbies, travel, and local cultural events. And a number of them continue to work part-time while participating in the activities of the LIR.

The desire to affiliate with an LIR also was not the result of taking advanced work in a specific discipline. If an applicant did want to join in order to enroll in an upper-level course, he or she would have been told quite early on that the program did not offer advanced studies. Nor were the potential members trying to take courses so that they could advance in their careers, those being largely completed. Few members had any desire to go back to college to be traditional students again, and fewer yet thought of themselves as scholars with a thirst for continuing scholarly activities.

If not for social or academic reasons, why were they applying for admission to the LIR? The reasons varied. Many, on joining, were uncertain about what they would like to study. Most had a vague feeling that they were not exercising their minds to the fullest, and that the LIR might provide them with an opportunity to do so. Many others held a deep-seated, pervasive sense of unease that time was slipping by but they were standing still.

A fair number said they had been keeping busy with volunteer work in a social agency or hospital. Others were taking continuing education courses at a local college or through Elderhostel, or traveling, or playing golf. Some had started new hobbies. With all that, however, they sensed in retirement a lack of purpose and usefulness to what they were doing. There existed a psychological void produced by a lessening of intellectual and social stimuli. Yes, they had been keeping busy, but they had not been getting any fun out of all the activity.

Somehow, the pleasures of leisure-time retirement living that they had anticipated proved inadequate. Something seemed to have been lost in the transition. Many discovered that they missed the psycho-social satisfactions that their job had provided. That job (when it was satisfactory) was more than salary: It provided an informal social network of colleagues with whom they could relate on matters both general and intimate. The network gave them a built-in support in times of difficulty, and a source of intelligent conversation. The job, in short, encompassed a system of belonging, wherein acceptance could be assured. What many missed most in retirement was the friends and colleagues from the workplace.

The job also provided a structure, and helped organize the day. It provided a time and place to be somewhere to do something specific. There was safety and security, not only in the salary but in the certainty of order. It was a place where you could put your hat—every day. The job also reinforced a feeling of self-worth. They knew their work was important and useful, that they were good at it, and that they were contributing members of society. They felt that colleagues respected them for work well done. More than prestige and purposefulness, though, the job provided them opportunities to keep their minds working. New developments in their field of work were always being introduced, and they were expected to keep up with them. There was always something new to learn.

The greatest job satisfaction came for many when they were praised by employers and colleagues for having created or developed a change in practice or thinking that affected the firm, the company, the business, or the profession. These creative moments of self-actualization, too rarely realized, provided high points of living. In retirement, outside of the job, LIR applicants did not find the psycho-social satisfactions they needed. Their hobbies, recreational activities, travel, and volunteer work, while useful, did not give them the needed gratifications. Their conscious or subconscious hope was that the LIR could.

Intellectual Benefits

Among the important benefits that participants in member-driven programs like to talk about are the opportunities for exploring new intellectual interests—which can vary from that of the retired dentist who finds that he wants to write short stories, to the choice of the former supermarket manager who discovers new interests in the geology of his state. The excitement of this intellectual search was well expressed by participants in the "Five College Learning in Retirement Program" in western Massachusetts (Amherst, Hampshire, Mount Holyoke, Smith, and the University of Massachusetts) when they wrote:

> We are a group of intellectually restless grown-up men and women who are now free to pursue new fields of study, re-ponder old neglected ones, and share, thereby reshape, familiar ideas with peers of diverse backgrounds and experiences who also remain intellectually independent and alert but who wish to join with others in the joy of learning.... We are doctors, lawyers, merchants, fire chiefs, educators, homemakers, artists, journalists, psychologists. We are engineers who want to read poetry; we are biologists, eager to commit history.

A somewhat more dramatic expression of the excitement of new learning took place at an open house at The New School's "Institute for Retired Professionals" (IRP). One speaker, a German refugee, told the guests what the IRP meant to him. He joined IRP because he thought it might be fun to take part in a German literature program conducted solely in German. His interest was not the literature, but the opportunity to speak German—something he missed badly. Shortly after joining, he attended a session of the "Philosophical Explorations" study-group because a friend of his was presenting a paper there. He then liked the easy way the members dealt with philosophical questions, and decided to stay with the group. After attending for several months, he was asked to lead a discussion the following semester on "Aesthetics of Photography," his lifetime hobby. This was the catalyst that helped him become fully involved; it was his first experience with academic research. Preparing his presentation, he said, was one of the most demanding but enjoyable tasks he had ever undertaken. He is still at it, reading books, and taking courses under regular New School faculty. For him, the Institute means intellectual excitement and stimulation.

Finding new fields of study is not the only intellectually exciting element of LIR programs. Of equal importance is the opportunity that members have to share personal experiences, and to deepen their insights and understanding of the changes that have taken place in their lifetime, and indeed in their lives. Such experiential study covers all courses, but is most strongly felt in literature and the humanities.

How can members of LIRs give meaning to their experiences of major world and national events which occurred in their adulthood? The Great Depression. World War II. The rise and fall of Communist states. The growth of an aging society. The change in family makeup. The technological revolution in communication. Advances in medicine. The nuclear threat. Four and five career changes in a lifetime. And lots more.

All LIR members have stories to tell of how each of these major world events affected their lives. Few people outside the LIR, however, have taken the opportunity to reflect on the *meanings* of these serious events. In the LIR, however, because of its open and nurturing atmosphere, it becomes possible for members to deal seriously with the impact of such experiences. In a significant way, too, the experiential learning that is basic to the philosophy of most programs is best when it takes place by means of discussion among persons who have lived through the same events. It cannot be as effective in an intergenerational group. It is impossible in a lecture format. Most of all, it requires the nonjudgmental character of the LIRs. The thought is well expressed by a member of the Springfield College LIR when she says:

> I never realized it before when I was teaching college students, but peer teaching is altogether different than teaching with younger students. Older students are more enthusiastic, involved and interested. Also, when I'm with older adults I'm an equal, not "The Teacher." Age is a great leveler.... In an Institute classroom, it's more of a knowledge-sharing situation, and there is no such barrier. These people are my friends, and we learn from each other.

For LIR members (and older people generally) a supportive environment is essential. The creative talents of members can come to the fore much more effectively in such an atmosphere. With it, members can and do undertake tasks and suggest solutions to problems that they would not dare if they were not certain that their efforts would be taken seriously—even if not accepted—by members of their group. As a result, members who "couldn't draw a straight line" are now exhibiting their art work in shows; others who were sure they had no talent for writing are having their poems and stories published; and some who never could understand the relevance of history are presenting research reports in their classes on such topics as "The Role of Women in the Middle Ages."

Social Benefits

With few exceptions, when participants in member-driven programs are asked what they are getting out of their program, they tell of the friendships formed, the camaraderie of members, the informal social network to which they belong, and the support received in times of difficulty. A member of the "Center for Learning in Retirement" (CLIR) at the University of California, Berkeley, says it for thousands of other members: "CLIR is important to me; it's a second family, a place to find friends and to learn."

To a considerable extent, the LIR provides a social network that substitutes well for that of the workplace. This new network, based on a common interest in learning, provides a setting in which the human need for belonging and love can be met. In the midst of losses that becoming older can bring (for example, losses among family and friends), the ability to meet new people of the same age and experience, within the framework of a university, can be enormously gratifying.

Relations among LIR members go beyond interests of academic matters or common events of the day. They touch the deeper concerns, as when joy wants to be shared, and when support is needed in times of grief or sadness. Typical, perhaps, is the short note in the *Newsletter* of Northwestern's "Institute for Learning in Retirement" (Evanston, Illinois):

> Being a member of the ILR is wonderful. The joys are many—walking the campus, exchanging ideas, meeting new people, using a brain that may have gone dormant, laughing, and of course, lunch. I have experienced all the above and more. Recently I broke my kneecap. I required surgery and I was hospitalized for two days. The warmth and caring and concern that so many of you have given me cannot be measured. Your friendship warms my heart. Yes, ILR is much more than its name implies.

As was noted earlier in this chapter, social activities are an important part of the LIR experience. They can include virtually anything, from end-of-term class parties and parties for religious events, to impromptu parties organized because someone's granddaughter graduated from college with honors. Other social events tied in with academic programs include one-day or overnight trips to nearby museums, exhibitions, plays, concerts, and/or ballets; and to nearby cities where their total cultural offerings can be sampled; and one- to three-week overseas study tours.

Of special importance to the LIR social life is the lunchroom or cafeteria, if either is available, where members can eat together. In a humorous essay, one of the members of The New School's LIR described the 125 or more members at lunch (where they occupy the cafeteria by themselves, and the decibel level sometimes rivals that of a small textile mill):

> The intellectual competition was intense. And nothing was haphazard. In the cafeteria there was a network of specialization—conservative tables, liberal tables, women's tables (sheer numbers caused this), men's tables (not chauvinistic, just the result of being an endangered species). Within each table there was further refinement of expertise. At the Marxist table, one member had the Nicaragua concession, another the Near East, and so on.

Most LIR directors and officers agree that the philosophy of *their* program mandates strong academic and social programs. Moreover, there is complete acceptance of the fact that as long as there is an appropriate balance between the two, and the directors and officers believe there is, each is a strong support for the other. No matter the specific philosophy, however: It is unlikely that any LIR would survive if its academic program was not augmented with a social program, or if its social program was not heavily balanced by a serious academic program. The membership requires benefits in both.

Maintaining a Sense of Purpose and Usefulness

Participants who become actively involved in member-driven programs find themselves better able than before to maintain a sense of purposefulness and usefulness, an essential psycho-social need for older people. Such involvement, however, calls for more than merely sitting in on a discussion group or listening to a lecture. It calls for an action role in sharing the academic, social, and administrative work necessary to keep the program moving. Fortunately, many opportunities exist for members to find such work and demonstrate to themselves and others that they are still able to be effective members of the community.

LIR members gain the admiration and respect of colleagues, and raise their own self-evaluation, when they play useful and purposeful roles in the program. These can include serving as study-group leaders; presenting research papers they have prepared, which will be the basis for one of the class sessions; exhibiting one or more of their works in an art show; helping to prepare the program newsletter or bulletin; serving on one of the many committees; helping the office to get out the mail, or doing some typing; and/or completing all assignments in preparation for class sessions. Those members who are actively involved in making the LIR function tend to find much greater satisfaction in their LIR experience than those who limit themselves to attending classes.

There is purposeful and useful work enough for all, if members will look for it. An example is in one program of 600 members, typical perhaps of most large programs, where more than half of the members are actively involved in doing the work that makes the LIR function. Some 120 members serve as study-group leaders (many of the groups have more than one leader), most of whom also prepare class presentations. Another 125 members present research papers which serve as the basis for group discussion. About 60 other members, who neither lead groups nor present papers, exhibit their paintings, sculpture, needlecraft, or ceramic work at one or another of the art shows. Another 30, who are in none of the above categories, publish their poems, short stories, and essays in the literary journal. Finally, each of more than 35 members (not duplicated above) is actively involved with one of the nine standing committees, including the social committee (which handles the coffee and refreshments at the parties) and the office volunteers (who stuff envelopes, do typing, answer the phones, handle members' questions, and perform other administrative chores as called upon). Many other members enrich the discussions by voluntarily reading or writing well beyond the regular assignments.

In other LIRs, where programs are conducted in the wider university, members involved in counseling undergraduate or graduate students, or working with foreign students in an English as a Second Language program, feel a sense of pride in serving others. Where LIRs have an outreach program to senior centers or nursing homes, many members find great satisfaction in giving a talk, or performing, or leading a discussion group.

Members also recognize the useful role they play in raising funds for their own program, or for the wider university. Most LIRs have a scholarship fund to which members contribute for their own members, but at the Brooklyn College "Institute for Retired Professionals and Executives," members also raise funds for four undergraduate scholarships. In other LIRs, members are taking the lead in raising funds for a building which can be shared by both the LIR and the university. More than $2 million was raised by members at the University of Delaware for a $6 million building in Wilmington which will be shared by both the "Academy of Lifelong Learning" and the university. At the University of California–Fullerton, members raised a similar amount for a building shared by the LIR and the college. A similar fund-raising program also was initiated at Harvard University.

Controlling Your Life

One of the important innate needs of older persons is to feel that they are sufficiently in control of their lives to function effectively in the wider society. One way they can experience this is to have a major role in making the decisions that affect them. Often, however, they are frustrated, in their efforts to maintain control, by stereotypes which picture the elderly as incapable of handling matters by themselves, and by well-meaning family and professionals (including educators) who feel they are better able to decide what older people want than are the older people themselves.

In face of pressures from those who, with of course the best of intentions, want to ease the burdens of members by making decisions for them, most of the members regularly affirm their capacity to make their own decisions—or, at the least, to negotiate differences with the administrators with whom they work. When they succeed in so doing, it provides them with the satisfaction of knowing that they are still fully functioning, and the confidence that the faith they had in themselves was justified. Where decision-making is taken away from them, they are in their own mind diminished. Within LIRs this search for control can sometimes create problems. On the one hand, the opportunity that members have to control decisions on academic offerings is a source of considerable gratification. On the other hand, the need to conform to the sponsor's requirements on matters of budget and fees can create a sense of repression.

Robert Atchley (1983) notes that if older people are to cope successfully with the negative images of aging that surround them in the media, and with well-meaning but ineffectual people who insist on "helping," it frequently is necessary for the elderly to defend themselves through interacting with others. Much of this interacting can be done in member-driven LIRs, which provide a built-in mechanism for allowing members to maintain a degree of control in the important educational growth area of their life. As stated by a member of the Harvard "Institute for Learning in Retirement" (Cambridge, Massachusetts):

> What I feared most when I retired was the loss of companionship of the intelligent, vital people with whom I had been working. HILR has replaced my old companions with a new, larger, and even more enthusiastic group of friends with whom I have explored many fields of knowledge over the past six years, and my future with HILR seems boundless in opportunities for new friendships, new explorations, and new interests.

Clearly, of major importance to members is the ability to decide for themselves which courses they want to take, and to have a share in deciding what will be included in the courses. Recognition of their competence to help shape the general curriculum reinforces a positive self-image. Members who do not want to be actively involved in the shaping of curriculum can nevertheless help elect officers and counselors who will represent their views on the LIR's operation. At all times these members will be solicited for their ideas as to the direction the program should take, and this too can provide gratification if they immediately and carefully respond to the solicitations.

A study by Elderhostel of how LIR members who attended Elderhostel programs felt about both programs indicated that LIR members had high praise for both the Elderhostel programs and the sponsoring colleges and institutions. They spoke of the friendliness of participants, and the level of academic rigor in Elderhostel programs. But, they emphasized, Elderhostel was someone else's program; it belonged to the college and Elderhostel. Administrators, not participants made all the educational decisions. The LIR was different: It belonged to the members. Not only was there pride of ownership, but the sense of being in control of the total operation—of being able to make decisions affecting their own educational life—was most salutary.

Health and Income Benefits

Most participants in member-driven programs are among the physically well, elderly, and middle-income group. They may take innumerable pills, have arthritis, and suffer from a variety of chronic ailments, but for the most part they are ambulatory—they drive themselves, or take public transportation, to class. Although they do not join the LIR for health reasons, it is quite common to hear many of them observe that they feel much better because of their LIR activities.

Credence for such anecdotal reporting comes from Dr. Ellen Langer, professor of psychology at Harvard University, whose long research with frail elderly on the positive impact of an active mind on physical and mental health is detailed in her book *Mindfulness* (1989). Her findings show that not only can there be remission of various ailments, but life expectancy can be increased, for nursing-home patients—if greater intellectual demands are made of them. Her research results indicate that by using the same techniques, illnesses for other age groups could be shortened. She writes:

> In one recent experiment we gave arthritis sufferers various interesting word problems to increase their mental activity. For example, subjects in this group were given slightly doctored sayings such as "a bird in the bush is worth two in the hand," and were asked to explain them. Comparison subjects were given the old familiar versions. In the mindful group, not only did subjective measures of comfort and enjoyment change, but some of the chemistry of the disease (sedimentation rates of the blood in this case) was affected as well. There were no significant changes in the comparison group.

Expressing the same sense of the health-giving qualities of intellectual rigor in an LIR setting is the statement of Dr. Jeremy Rusk (1985), founder and first director of the Harvard LIR:

> What does it [Harvard's "Institute for Learning in Retirement"] produce? Intellectual excitement. Good health. I am convinced that programs of this kind could be demonstrated over the long run to have had a positive, productive effect on the Gross National Product in saved medical expenses alone. I am certain that there are people who are alive right now because they are members of the Institute. . . . The Institute looks to me like a sort of secular church, a genuine fellowship.

However, not depending on their academically rigorous classes alone to shorten their illnesses or lengthen their lives, members of most medium and large LIRs have added a variety of physical fitness and nutrition programs to their curriculums. Thus, for example, between their classes in philosophy, science, and literature, the members of Temple University's "Association for Retired Professionals" have added to their curriculum classes on "Easy Exercises," "Jazzy Exercises," and "Modern Nutrition"; Brooklyn College's LIR members have opted to include, in their basically academic program, classes in "Slimnastics" and "Dieting Dynamics"; and members of American University's "Institute for Learning in Retirement" have added to their intellectually demanding program courses in "No-Nonsense Nutrition" and "Exercise."

In a number of instances, sponsoring colleges provide members—at no cost or at a reduced fee—courses leading to new careers, and consultation services for members thinking of starting new careers. With some exceptions, however, member interest in exploring new career options represents a search for additional ways to gratify unmet psycho-social needs, rather than to supplement inadequate current income.

However, some members have expressed a desire to increase incomes by scheduling courses in investment techniques. These range from "Investing in Local Opportunities" at the Duke Institute, to "Financial Planning Workshops" at the Institute at California State University–Fullerton. (No research has been conducted to determine whether these or other investment courses have in fact increased income.) The late Dr. Edwin Buxbaum, founding member of the "Academy of Lifelong Learning" at the University of Delaware, summed up the feeling of most LIR members when he said "The Academy is not only a club, it is a church, it is a clinic, but most importantly, it is a college."

PART III

Expanded Visions and New Horizons in the Third Age

Presuppositions and stereotypes about retirement and later life have changed and are changing. LIRs have been instrumental in demonstrating the capacity of older adults to assume responsibility for their own learning and to take control and shape the value of later life for themselves and society.

8

Intergenerational Synergy

JAMES K. BROOMALL

Age-integrated learning provides opportunities for adult development to be facilitated by interaction across developmental life stages. This is consistent with the view that human development occurs along an age continuum which is not rigidly demarcated by chronological age. The synergy occurs from the combining of the experience of older adults with the enthusiasm and energy of youth.

This chapter briefly examines the concept of intergenerational learning and its contemporary institutional applications. The primary intent is to outline the nature of age-integrated programming in contrast with age-segregated activity. Particular attention is given to applications of the concept in varied settings as consistent with the general theme of this text, to meet the needs of practitioners and contribute to the professional literature. Since intergenerational learning is an emergent idea, institutional case studies are of course limited. Nevertheless, they adequately manifest the idea as applied in diverse contexts.

A significant participation or membership pattern in learning-in-retirement programming is age-segregated enrollment. In fact, the institutionalized approach to education for older learners is dominated by this approach. That is, participation as an instructor or student is limited to people within a specifically designated age category. For example, the University of Delaware's "Academy of Lifelong Learning" limits membership to adults of age

55 or older and their spouses, while "The Plato Society" of UCLA limits enrollment to those aged 50 or older with 20 years of business, professional, artistic, or volunteer experience. Typical arguments in support of age-segregated programming include ". . . low cost, the informal/social nature of the classroom, and the relevance of the content to participants' interests" (Peterson, 1983). Of course, the social dimension is particularly important in the age-segregated approach as participants form a cohort characterized by shared interests and experiences. This approach is consistent with the andragogical model of program development suggested by Knowles (1973) and applied in various adult education endeavors. Yet, as Peterson (1983) and others (Courtenay, 1989; Long, 1983) suggest, it is problematic whether age-segregated programming for older adult learners achieves optimum learner satisfaction or is indeed the preferred approach.

A review of several institutions' catalogues that describe learning-in-retirement programs indicates that age-segregated programs share several distinct characteristics. A primary element is that such programs generally are sponsored by two-year and four-year colleges and universities. Second, the members constitute a common age cohort generally defined at some given point such as age 55 and older. In fact, some institutions, such as The New School for Social Research's "Institute for Retired Professionals" (IRP), more finely define admission. IRP restricts admission to retired professionals. Third, programming is offered on a noncredit basis and generally is administered as either a free-standing administrative unit, a program within a continuing education division or school, or some cooperative variation thereof. Fourth, the curriculum is staffed by and enrolled in by individuals from the membership's age cohort. The members develop the courses, teach them, serve on committees, and plan enrichment and outreach activities. Some sponsoring colleges allow program members to enroll in credit courses and degree options on a space-available basis. However, this varies across institutions. A final characteristic is that the programs are financially self-supported by membership dues, and therefore are subject to market considerations in recruitment and selection.

Age-integrated approaches to learning-in-retirement programs also are generally offered under the rubric of two-year and four-year colleges and universities. However, they differ markedly from age-segregated programming in several ways. First, a given educational experience will enroll students across the age continuum. Standards for admission are defined by the sponsoring institution and are not determined chronologically. Second, programming is offered in both credit and noncredit formats. A third element is that courses are staffed by regular full-time and part-time faculty. The curriculum generally follows the discipline or problem-centered approach of other institutional activity. Fourth, programming generally is not offered by a distinct administrative unit. Rather, participants enroll in courses and programs offered throughout the institution. In a sense, older learners are "mainstreamed" into the broader fabric of the institution.

Intergenerational Learning: A Working Definition

Peterson (1983, p. 302) suggests the need to explore intergenerational learning: "An issue to be addressed in the future is whether older students should be included in the future in course work for younger learners, whether older learners are so distinct as to justify programs designed exclusively for them, or whether there should be some new form of course work that is designed for age-integrated audiences." The focus in programming of this nature is interaction across the age continuum. Peacock and Tally (1984) outline a working definition of intergenerational learning that can be applied to a myriad of settings and across different educational interests. To them, "Intergenerational activity, loosely defined, suggests the interaction of all age groups, infant to elderly, in a variety of situations at a level that provides a close communication, sharing of feelings and ideas, and cooperative activity in meaningful tasks." Peacock and Talley (1984, p. 13), Sprouse (1982), Long (1983), and Courtenay (1989) emphasize the positive attitudes of older learners to age-integrated programming.

A working definition of intergenerational learning includes five fundamental elements:

1. The experience involves a group of older learners interacting with one or more other age cohorts. This can be elementary or secondary school students, traditional college-age students, or middle-age learners.

2. The educational intent varies according to institutional goals. For example, the focus can be community service, emotional support, or academic instruction.

3. Programming characteristics regarding curriculum, staffing, and budgeting are not the exclusive province of the older learners. Rather, they generally are determined by the institutional sponsor.

4. Decisions regarding admissions, participation, and/or membership are not the responsibility of the older learner but instead are determined by the sponsoring institution.

5. Regardless of the instructional vehicle, the goal of facilitating a sense of shared awareness and sensitivity across the age continuum remains in the forefront.

While the educational intent or programming methods may vary, the common intent in intergenerational learning is to promote intellectual and emotional interaction across/between generations.

Adult Development: Ages and Stages

The concept of adult lifespan development provides a sound theoretical framework within which to explore intergenerational learning. Pioneered in the research by Havighurst (1972) and Erikson (1963) and popularized by Levinson (1974) and others, this model of human development defines adulthood as a series of age-related stages with associated developmental tasks. Integral to adult development theory is the assumption that these stages occur on a continuum along which one passes through various stages of personality development and physical change culminating in old age (Peterson, 1983). Knox (1977) also emphasizes the sequential nature of this development. Since these stages occur throughout a continuous life pattern, successful completion of the tasks associated with one age-related stage ensures fuller development in subsequent stages.

Synthesizing the research related to adult development, Weathersby (1977; 1978) outlines a useful characterization of life phases in adult development. According to Weathersby, each life phase or stage confronts the adult with major psychic tasks, marker events, and characteristic stance. Weathersby cites a generalized developmental series of life phases: First, the adult leaves the family (16–18 to 20–24 years) and then, during the early 20s to late 20s, enters into the adult world. During the age 30 transition the adult begins to question, "What do I want out of life?" While the early 30s are a time of "settling down," the late 30s involve greater personal integration. Midlife transition occurs during the early 40s with restabilization following around age 45–50. For Weathersby, adults in the late 50s and early 60s are in a period of "mellowing and flowering," in which opportunities to pursue varied interests are valued. Accomplishments are personally defined, not weighed against socially determined norms. The 60s and beyond are a time to review life's choices.

Age-segregated programming is designed to enable those in a defined developmental stage to participate in a common educational experience. However, Chickering (1969) suggests that traditional college-age students (i.e., 18- to 24-year-olds) experience similar phases of adult development in their movement toward self-identify and integration. Referring to this population, he writes: "Developmental changes do occur during this period. Numerous cross-sectional and longitudinal studies of college students indicate that changes occur in attitudes, interests, values, future plans, and aspirations, openness to impulse and emotions, personal integration, and intellectual ability" (1969, p. 2). The challenge that these younger adult learners face is to develop a valid set of beliefs and value constructs to guide their subsequent development. In fact, a significant part of the collegiate experience is devoted to this end (Chickering, 1981).

Perry (1970) also emphasizes the critical nature of development among college-age students in both the intellectual and emotional spheres. Their focus is on both "knowing" and "valuing." College-age students' development moves from basic dualistic morality (i.e., absolutism) through relativism to moral commitment. Perry contends, "In education, such a developmental scheme would promise relevance to procedure of selection, curriculum design, classroom teaching, and advising" (Perry, 1970, p. 15; Jacob, 1957; Katz, 1962), and others address the developmental approach to understanding college-age students.

Older adult learners obviously face different developmental tasks from their traditional college-age counterparts. However, they are moving through a common experience of valuing and questioning. The socialization function of higher education clearly emphasizes the role of peer-group support in this process. Intergenerational learning provides a ripe opportunity for adult development to be facilitated by interaction across developmental stages. This is consistent with the view of lifelong learning and adult development as occurring along a continuum which is not rigidly demarcated by chronological age.

Intergenerational Learning: Program Characteristics and Institutional Applications

Intergenerational learning occurs within several organizational contexts. Elementary and secondary schools (Corbin, Kagan, and Corbin, 1987; Sparling and Rogers, 1985); community-based service organizations (Peacock and Talley, 1984); and two-year and four-year colleges and universities (Firman, Gelfand, and Ventura, 1983; Long, 1983) all are involved in intergenerational programming. Consistent with the general focus of this volume, attention here is paid to activities within a postsecondary education environment.

College and university involvement in intergenerational learning generally has one of two major forms. The first is academic programming geared toward intellectual/cognitive development. The second is community service programming directed toward emotional/affective development *or* contribution to the greater social good. In each case learners from the several age cohorts (i.e., traditional 18–24-year-old college students, returning middle-age participants, and older adult learners) join together for a common educational experience. Through the process intergenerational learning contributes to the diversity and richness of the campus environment (Moyer and Logo, 1987).

Intergenerational learning has not been institutionalized to the same extent as age-segregated programming. However, there are some examples of application of the concept. Institutional applications are categorized according to one of two major intents: intellectual development through academic programming, or emotional development.

INTELLECTUAL DEVELOPMENT

Academic programming which promotes intergenerational learning often involves older adults in regular college classes or promotes their interaction with traditional college-age students through mentoring or teaching. Eckerd College's "Academy of Senior Professionals" (ASPEC) illustrates this approach. Eckerd College is a coeducational private liberal-arts college in St. Petersburg, Florida. Learning-in-Retirement program membership is open to retired or semiretired men and women with distinguished careers in the professions or other fields of endeavor. Members interact with undergraduate students and faculty as discussant colleagues in certain courses and through international education activities. Particular focus is on involving older learners with younger learners through mentoring. A degree completion program for adults is available through the "Program for Experiential Learning (PEL). Eckerd was awarded a grant in 1991 from the Fund for the Improvement of Postsecondary Education (FIPSE) to promote intergenerational learning through interaction between PEL and ASPEC members.

Another program of note is Fairleigh Dickinson University's Florham–Madison Campus "Educational Program for Older Adults." Fairleigh Dickinson is a multicampus comprehensive university located in northern New Jersey. Designed for adults age 65 and over, the tuition-free educational and social program combines age-integrated with age-segregated programming. Members can enroll in undergraduate and graduate degree credit courses on a space-available basis. A related department, "Development of Life Experience," offers specially designed courses. Approximately 175 learners participate in the program each semester.

Through the North Carolina "Center for Creative Retirement," The University of North Carolina–Asheville (UNCA) sponsors "College for Seniors," which includes intergenerational learning. UNCA is a comprehensive constituent university within the University of North Carolina system. Selected noncredit liberal-arts courses offered in the "College for Seniors" also enroll undergraduate students. Intergenerational learning occurs as well through "The Senior Academy" by involving older adults as mentors, career advisers, and lecturers for traditional college-age students.

At UCLA, "The Plato Society" affords an opportunity for undergraduate honors students to interact with Society members in group discussion. Undergraduates can earn "honors credit" through mutual study with "retiree scholars" involved in independent learning. Society members can demonstrate their diverse life and professional experiences, and have them evaluated from another generational perspective. This exemplifies a highly selective approach to intergenerational learning.

Kingsborough Community College's "My Turn" is a tuition-free program open to New York State residents of age 65 and older. Kingsborough, part of The City University of New York, is an urban, comprehensive community college located in Brooklyn. Membership is determined exclusively by age and residence; one can be retired, employed, unemployed, or never employed. Program participants enroll in degree credit courses offered throughout the regular academic year, and are integrated with the regular student body. The "My Turn" curriculum mirrors that of the regular undergraduate Kingsborough offerings, so older learners can carry as few or as many credits each semester as they want. Upon completion of 24 credits in "My Turn" one can earn the General Education Development (GED) diploma from the New York State Department of Education. Although older learners enroll in regular classes, they can also attend special enrichment and counseling programs. "My Turn" members demonstrate to younger students the intrinsic value of learning for its own sake.

In Canada, Toronto's Ryerson Polytechnical Institute "Program in Intergenerational Education" (PIE) promotes learning across the age continuum. PIE's agenda includes participation in policy development, and project stimulation and development. It assists educators and social workers interested in organizing their own intergenerational programs. Other Canadian endeavors include Seniors in School (SIS), which pairs older adults and children in a neighborhood school in Vancouver.

The most common institutional approach to intergenerational learning in academic programming occurs through tuition-waiver options. However, these generally restrict enrollment to a space-available basis. Intergenerational learning may occur through the spontaneous communication among class members. But no special arrangements are made, since the academic discipline or subject area under consideration drives the curriculum. Nevertheless, available studies indicate that older learners perform as well as younger students; social relations in the classroom also have proved positive (Long, 1983). Personal anecdotes abound of elder learners who complete traditional undergraduate or graduate degrees.

EMOTIONAL DEVELOPMENT

Community service programming which promotes intergenerational learning draws older learners and others together in some form of shared experience. Western Washington University's Fairhaven College, a cluster campus of 500 students within the university, exemplifies this approach. Western Washington is a comprehensive university in Bellingham, Washington. Through "the Bridge at Bellingham," a preschool playground is connected with an apartment building whose residents generally are aged 55 and older. Four distinct age cohorts are involved in social interaction: preschool children; those of ages 5–11 enrolled in a cooperative school; Western Washington degree candidates who range in age from the late teens to the forties; and older adults. The major program focus is to involve older adults with others of different ages through social interaction via a residential experience.

Since 1980, Temple University's Institute on Aging has sponsored "The Center for Intergenerational Learning." Temple is an urban research university located in Philadelphia. The Center's programming includes service-oriented projects in schools, child-care centers, nursing homes, senior centers, community organizations, churches, and synagogues. The interaction among age cohorts is directed toward the solution of particular social problems. For example, traditional college-age students serve as tutors in basic reading and writing skills for older adults. Another project involves retired workers as teachers, tutors, and mentors for high school students enrolled in vocational courses offered by the Philadelphia School District. Temple's program is designed to encourage learners of different ages to explore social issues common to both groups. A similar approach is evident in Kansas State University extension programs on grandparenting. Children and older adult learners interact in such programs as "Generations Together" and "Grandletters."

Several trends emerge from the case studies outlined here:

1. The sponsoring institution more than the participants plays a major role in the educational design for intergenerational learning. In academic programming the traditional curriculum provides the nexus for interaction between/among generations. Programs oriented to emotional development center around community service topics. Age-segregated programs generally are member-driven in the educational design.

2. Successful group dynamics are critical to intergenerational learning. Whether the method is an academic discipline or a project, the key remains the structure of interaction among the age cohorts.

3. The limited available research indicates that older and younger learners both find intergenerational experiences to be emotionally and academically satisfying (Long, 1983).

4. Institutional involvement in intergenerational learning is significantly less than that in age-segregated programming. A possible explanation may be that age-integrated programming affords participants less autonomy. As a result, institutional decision-making may give intergenerational learning a low priority.

Conclusion

The role of intergenerational learning in the broader learning-in-retirement movement remains problematic. From a conceptual standpoint, intergenerational learning realizes the ideals of the lifelong learning continuum. Learners of all ages interact to explore academic topics and/or issues of social significance. Despite differences in age and developmental stage, the learners address issues of mutual concern common to the quest for intellectual and emotional integrity.

There is little empirical research on the outcomes of intergenerational learning programs. A topic for future research in this area is the differences in participant satisfaction, attitude changes, and knowledge acquired in age-integrated versus age-segregated programming. The differences in group dynamics between age-integrated and age-segregated programming is a related research topic. As there is heightened program activity in the realm of intergenerational learning, the opportunities for systematic investigation also will increase. This may demonstrate more vividly the similarities and differences between age-integrated and age-segregated programming.

The "age wave" discussed in other chapters in this book, and the response from the higher education community, will alter the direction of learning-in-retirement programming during the 1990s. Age-segregated programs will undoubtedly build upon the financial and enrollment successes of the 1970s and 1980s and continue to expand. Yet, intergenerational learning's role needs further definition. The extent to which older learners are willing to have decreased autonomy in programming decisions, and to be "mainstreamed" into the institutional fabric, remains an unanswered but vital question as we approach the year 2000. An affirmative response from learning-in-retirement programs and institutions will diminish ageism and provide an opportunity for enriched intellectual and emotional development of all age groups involved.

9

Creative Retirement in an Aging Society

RONALD J. MANHEIMER

The proliferation of LIRs indicates that higher education is increasingly serving multigenerational audiences. This increases the need to reexamine how life stages are interrelated and how colleges can help older adults find new roles.

The Third-Age Learner in an Aging Society

George Kriedler played pro football for the Green Bay Packers. That was in 1939. He played baseball for the Army leagues in 1944 after he was commandeered into a jeep off a beach in North Africa and transported to Baltimore to play third base. Returning to school after the war, George was trained as an engineer, eventually working for Bechtel. He resumed his education at the age of 56 to study management. Bechtel put him in charge of hundreds of workers at nuclear power plant construction sites. He continued to play ball, from the sidelines, as a little-league coach. After retiring, Kriedler went back to school again at the University of North Carolina–Asheville's (UNCA's) North Carolina Center for Creative Retirement (NCCCR). He could have been taking courses in the center's peer-learning and teaching program, "College for Seniors." But that season he was again serving as a coach—to an undergraduate baseball player. He wasn't advising about batting or catching, but about the work life of an engineer and a manager, the ball player's future double career goal.

Kriedler is one of the NCCCR's senior counselors in a program called SAIL, the "Senior Academy for Intergenerational Learning." His special project for SAIL is to serve, along with nineteen other retirees meeting one-on-one with UNCA athletes, to help make sure the ball players finish college with skills they can also use off the courts and playing fields. Like many of his fellow counselors, Kriedler enjoys and respects athletics and relates well to younger athletes. He's also had enough experience to know that a person's career is subject to surprises and changes, adaptation to new technologies and organizational innovations, and the need for periodic return to the classroom. His undergraduate athlete knows this, too: He's twenty-three years old and trying to balance finishing his degree with holding down a part-time job.

The demographic world of the third-age student is an aging society wherein the average American is now 33 years old. This phenomenon is reflected on college campuses, no longer the haven of 18- to 22-year-olds, where now the nontraditional age student is in the majority. Such students set a premium on applicable knowledge, and value the opportunity to explore career ideas with people like George Kriedler. And for some third-age students, such as Kriedler, lifelong learning is turning into lifelong teaching in the form of mentoring, tutoring, or advising. The strategic location of centers for learning in retirement (colleges and universities) gives them a special opportunity to transform senior learners into senior mentors or colleagues. This challenges them to find new roles that American society, for one, critically needs.

The story of the two ball players, young and old, illustrates the importance of thinking about senior adult learning in the broader context of education and society. It is the thesis of this chapter that as centers for learning in retirement proliferate, they will benefit by recognizing a societal mission as well as a personal enrichment one. Moreover, these centers may discover linkages to other program areas that help maximize well-being and productivity among third-age learners: areas such as leadership development, health promotion, intergenerational learning, and outreach to less formally educated seniors and those in rural areas. These developments will be part of daily life in an aging society and will correspond to changes in institutional and governmental public policy, redefinition of the meaning of retirement, and reconceptualization of how life's stages are interrelated. (One example portending these changes is the aforementioned NCCCR, which promotes educational enrichment for senior adults, and their participation in community service both on and off the campus. The center pursues this dual mission through eight multifaceted programs whose aspects are mutually enhancing.)

A quartet of hypotheses about the near future underlies the center's mission. *First:* The U.S., like many European countries, is moving toward an age-integrated society. In such societies the generations will be more interdependent and interactive than ever before. *Second:* Institutions of higher education will serve multigenerational audiences as adults of varying ages move in and out of college environments for different types of learning. *Third:* Fully- or semiretired individuals will be needed to provide continuity and guidance to a shrinking, younger-age work force. *Fourth:* A new consensus will emerge on the special purpose and meaning of later life that will give positive definition and shape to the roles of older adults. It is in the context of these hypotheses that activities of a creative retirement center can best be understood.

A Place for Creative Retirement

Creativity in the retirement years means, for some, active continuation of lifelong interests (perhaps in modified forms), and for others a reevaluation process possibly leading to a journey down what previously was "the road not taken." In either case adaptability, flexibility, and a belief that one's future is yet to be fashioned are characteristics of an innovative third quarter of life. The very notion that the terms "creativity" and "older adult" could be used in the same sentence has only recently emerged.

Harry Moody (1977, 1988) has reviewed changing attitudes or "philosophical presuppositions" of older adult education. He notes five chronological stages indicative of changing attitudes toward later life. *One:* Seniors neither need nor deserve more learning opportunities (rejection stage). *Two:* Education for seniors can be of special therapeutic value (social work stage). *Three:* Older adults are no different from other age groups and should be mainstreamed into existing educational pathways (normalization stage). *Four:* Learning in later life holds special transformative possibilities for personal growth (self-actualization stage). *Five:* Personal growth is inextricably bound up with social relations and community issues in which seniors should be empowered to participate (emancipation stage).

The evolution from the rejection stage to the self-actualization and emancipation stages has occurred over the past 30 years. A parallel to Moody's stages can be found in changing attitudes toward reminiscence. A social worker trained in the 1940s or early 1950s would have been instructed to discourage reminiscing among older people, since it was considered a form of pathology—a tendency to dwell in the past, indicating loss of contact with the present (Dobroff, 1984). By the late 1950s and early 1960s, researchers decided that reminiscing was part of a healthy universal "life review" process, a naturally occurring reckoning with one's life triggered by a growing awareness of one's mortality (Butler, 1963). By the early 1970s, some students from the humanistic school of gerontology (especially historians, philosophers, and artists) claimed that reminiscing held the potential for late-life creativity that could serve as the basis for renewal of the learning process. Wisdom, not senility, was wrapped up in memory (Kaminsky, 1984).

Despite this kind of radical reappraisal of later life and attention to the older learner's potential, there was little in the way of training that would allow educators to work easily with older people. Educational programs for third-agers occurred only sporadically, and at that mostly in the form of "demonstration" projects, many of which were funded by federal agencies such as the National Endowment for the Arts and the National Endowment for the Humanities, and their state-level counterparts. Despite enthusiastic claims of great success, these projects usually terminated at the end of their grant periods. Without outside money, most institutions closed senior-education programs. Attending to the educational needs of seniors was simply not high on the priority list for colleges, libraries, or even senior centers.

Following the gradual recovery from the post–Vietnam War recession, increasing numbers of nontraditional-age adults began to go back to school for both instrumental (vocational) and expressive (enrichment) purposes. Continuing education and lifelong learning became popular concepts, and many corporations began underwriting their employees' tuition fees. A hallmark of this trend came in 1976 when Congress passed the Lifelong Learning Act to support expansion of, and equitable access to, education for people of all ages. Despite the prominence of its main sponsor, then–Vice President Mondale, discord between education groups over who would get the largest share of the appropriation pie slowed momentum in Congress. The Act was never funded.

That same year saw the beginning of Elderhostel and The National Council on the Aging's (NCOA) Senior Center Humanities Program. Elderhostel was started to offer low-cost education and travel opportunities to those with limited financial means. But its phenomenal expansion came through participation of middle-class people, primarily retired professionals. The NCOA program, providing humanities reading and discussion kits based on the program's original anthologies, also grew rapidly, reaching yearly some 40,000 by 1984, a large portion of whom were, in fact, people with less than eight years of formal education (Manheimer, 1988). The New School's "Institute for Retired Professionals" (IRP) program had already been in existence for almost 20 years, but its impact on the growth of older adult education was still minimal, perhaps because for most places in the U.S. such a program was well before its time.

No single cause brought about the change in attitudes concerning older learners, or the expansion of institutionally based programs. Indeed a veritable spectrum of causal explanations can be given for the rise of third-age learning programs: sheer increase in the number of older adults (demographic explanation), increased market opportunities (economic explanation), the emergence of a new age cohort that was more affluent and better-educated than any before (sociological explanation), the growing organizational voice of seniors (political explanation), changing ideas about adult development and the purposes of later life (ideological explanation), and so on. Probably all of these factors contributed to the change. And the fact of growing numbers of senior learners and senior learning organizations as demonstrated in this volume indicates that the expansion is continuing, especially for those among the more privileged group of today's seniors. However, the problem of establishing a secure institutional base continues to challenge many programs, with the fee-driven member-based programs having the most promising futures.

Where does the North Carolina Center for Creative Retirement fit into this picture? The center's own birth came from the cross-fertilization of two ideas. The first resulted from a growing awareness of the large numbers of older adults migrating to western North Carolina, and their gradual surfacing on the campus. Shouldn't there be some kind of special continuing education program for these people? The second idea was bound up with a change in the very identity of UNCA. Under a new chancellor, long-simmering ambitions among faculty and administrators led to major plans for turning UNCA into an elite Ivy League kind of school that would remain financially accessible to the average student—a so-called public ivy. To foster this image, the school looked for curricular innovations that would be "distinctive," giving the school a special character and competitive edge. It found this, in part, in its 20-year commitment to an extensive humanities core curriculum required of all students; in undergraduate research projects; in intensifying collaborative learning among students and teachers; in remaining an intimate liberal-arts institution; and in launching an ambitious multiprogram center for older learners whose talents and resourcefulness also could augment the university's curricular goals.

The idea was not easy to sell. Some faculty members couldn't see the point of such a center—it was frivolous and, even worse, would drain campus resources already under strain. Some felt that serving seniors' educational needs lay outside the university's goals, or that older learners did not need a special age-segregated institute; they could simply enroll in regular campus courses. Others felt it distracted from the school's main purpose, which was to offer younger people a high-quality liberal-arts education. "Younger people" at UNCA meant both the 18- to 22-year-olds and "adult" students, people in their mid-twenties to mid-thirties, many of whom worked and commuted to campus. Few faculty members or administrators had prior experience with older adult education, though the chancellor had been significantly involved in establishing the Scripts Gerontology Center at Miami University of Ohio, where he had been provost. Moreover, his wife had taken a degree in social gerontology at Miami, and was aware of programs such as The New School's IRP, and Harvard's and Duke's "Institutes for Learning in Retirement."

Marketing the idea of the center also involved talking with the region's politicians, the delegates to the general assembly, then in positions of considerable power in the state. They saw the center as an asset to the university's reputation—and recognized an element of economic enhancement to the region, since an influx of retirees meant both a stronger tax base and increased revenues to area businesses. But how could the idea be sold to the whole state assembly? Perhaps the center could serve as a laboratory for the entire state, developing model programs that could be exported to towns and counties in the Piedmont area, the coastal area, and other parts of North Carolina. This approach was both sensible and successful. The center received an annual appropriation of core funding from the state.

The first program, an intensive leadership seminar derived from existing community leadership programs, was launched. "Leadership Asheville Seniors" provided seven day-long sessions, meeting once every other week to familiarize newcomers and longtime senior residents of their community's history, problems, needs, and opportunities. By the seventh session, those about to become "alumni" of the program would be ready to choose the volunteer cause or entrepreneurial opportunity that captured their imagination. And they did. Several became "loaned executives" to the annual United Way campaigns. One, a retired banker with a love of classical music, took charge of fund-raising for the Asheville Symphony Society. Another recruited additional retirees for an ambitious project to establish a relocation and employment program for newly released prisoners. Yet another group started a school volunteer mentor program, rounding up 70 other retirees. Just recently, grants from the Z. Smith Reynolds and Mary Reynolds Babcock foundations have enabled the center to assist each of eight other North Carolina communities to start its own "Creative Seniors Leadership Program."

The second program, "College for Seniors," recruited volunteer teachers among retirees and found considerable talent in subjects ranging from geology to history to computers. Retired college presidents, scientists, physicians, academics, corporate executives, writers, and artists warmed to the opportunity to keep in touch with their fields and avocations and to share them with others. To begin to familiarize UNCA faculty with the "inner world" of older learners, an outstanding professor was invited each semester to offer a course. He or she would receive an honorarium for teaching.

There were 165 registered in the first semester, with five courses available (one given twice). By the third semester the enrollment had just about doubled. Moreover, membership fees paid in for joining the CFS (giving members parking permits and access to most undergraduate privileges such as library, discounts for cultural events, etc.) eventually made the CFS financially self-sufficient.

Other programs were added, including retirement planning seminars for individuals and businesses; a senior entrepreneurial group designed to work with small businesses; a "Wellness Works" health-promotion course cosponsored with one of the local hospitals (Memorial Mission Medical Center); an off-campus humanities discussion group program called "Life Journey" (funded by the North Carolina Humanities Council); a research institute that also organized national issues forums and brought in major national figures in fields related to aging and the economy, education, business, health and government; and, so on.

What gave uniqueness to the Center was not simply the proliferation of programs but the interrelationship of these areas. For example, volunteer discussion-group leaders for the "Life Journey" program were recruited and trained from among members, teachers, and students of the "College for Seniors." These people then led groups in senior centers, public libraries, retirement communities, and other community centers for older people less mobile, well-educated, or economically well-off than themselves. Of course, this also enhanced their own enjoyment of learning. The "wellness" course produced alumni who became "Wellness Ambassadors." They, in turn, took on projects such as Senior Wellness Day—which, in its first year, attracted over 300 seniors to a day-long workshop series on everything from stress management and the uses of humor, to low-fat, low-cost Italian cuisine. As university departments became aware of the rich talent pool among "College for Seniors" faculty, they found needed adjunct faculty, who were hired to teach both regular courses and areas of their specialization.

The center received funds from the Appalachian Regional Commission (ARC), a federal agency, to study the economic and social impact of in-migrating retirees on the region. Some 30 interviewers were recruited and trained. Half were undergraduates and half retirees from the center's programs.

In 1989, after a long process of planning, the "Senior Academy for Intergenerational Learning" (SAIL) was launched to match up, in a wide variety of projects, undergraduates with retirees having distinctive professional and civic experience. Most of the mentors selected for SAIL had participated in one or another of the center's programs. SAIL most clearly epitomized the philosophy of the center and linked it to both the university's purpose and image—support of undergraduate education, and innovative uniqueness as a high-quality, small public ivy. Through SAIL, the center has become a more integral part of the campus, and begun to enter into the daily life of undergraduate students and faculty members. Misinformation, rumor, jealousy, and prejudice about the center have been reduced through the SAIL program as students and faculty have had more direct contact with seniors. Indirectly, knowledge of the SAIL program has lead to greater awareness of the center's full range of initiatives, perhaps educating students and faculty to the self-actualization and emancipation stages of older adult education, and the potential impact of that education on members of other generations.

MOVING TOWARD AN AGE-INTEGRATED SOCIETY

In 1989 the state's General Assembly voted to appropriate funds for UNCA to build a 75,000-square-foot Intergenerational Center. The building is meant to serve multiple purposes, including housing offices and classrooms, and providing executive-quality conference space for the university, for groups choosing to rent space for meetings, and for larger regional or national conferences, and even trade shows. As with the original founders of the center, local representatives to the Assembly saw the Intergenerational Center playing a key role in economic development, since the facility would draw more conferences to an increasingly popular meeting place, enhance the reputation and improve the facilities of the university, and strengthen the NCCCR's ability to deliver programs to a growing audience—some of whom were drawn to the area *because of* the center's programs. The first unit of the center was scheduled for completion in 1994.

The Intergenerational Center symbolizes the web of motives and trends of an aging society. UNCA, like most other institutions of higher education, continues to experience a rise in the average age of its students (which at this writing was 27, the 10 percent enrollment of the "College for Seniors" not included in that average). More people in their thirties and forties are signing up for a new degree program, the Masters of Liberal Arts. Adding the expansion of center programs for people 50 and over, clearly the university has become a multigenerational environment. But, as Dr. James Broomall acknowledged in Chapter 8, the proximity of multigenerational learners does not automatically produce either collaborative education or interaction between young and old. Nor does it indicate the course of university policy with regard to institutional structuring. The new building will serve people of all ages, but will or should their co-presence produce a new kind of learning environment?

The question of a multigenerational university environment reflects a parallel question: How age-integrated will a society be in which middle-age and older adults predominate? In part the answer to these questions lies in how retirement itself is conceptualized. There are two trends taking place. In this period of corporate takeovers and international competition, many companies are choosing to streamline their work force by encouraging attractive early-out retirement programs. On the other hand, one hears increasingly of senior employees being invited back to serve as consultants, to work in training programs with younger employees, or to consider staying on until the company has found adequately seasoned replacements. Older employees do not seem to be as obsolete as they once were. In a postindustrial, information-based society, the older person represents a considerable investment in human capital—i.e., the accumulated knowledge and experience of how the world works. Retired individuals represent a formidable reinvestment of resources and productivity *if* they can be placed in appropriate roles.

To what extent will programs such as the NCCCR be able to provide a new type of mentor/learner to the university community? How powerful will such programs come to be? How accepted will older mentors/learners be on campus as they interact with 18- to 22-year-olds, or the 30- and 40-year-old students? These are some of the questions being researched. It is still too early to draw conclusions.

Rationale for the Future

Today's older persons are perhaps in a similar position to that of women in the 1970s. The women's movement, and changes in the economy, brought large numbers of women to college and university campuses where "reentry" or "women in transition" courses helped to prepare them to find their way through the curriculum. Stereotypes were recognized as primarily socially and culturally determined rather than fixed by "nature." Women were finding new roles and new strengths while academic scholarship was itself changed with the advent of women's studies and feminist criticism.

These developments have their parallels in the social and cultural history of aging. Though not in large numbers as yet, older people are gravitating to college communities as places for retirement *and* for continuing education. To varying degrees they are exploring new avenues and roles that have few precedents, if any. Retirement age no longer means a time primarily for leisure or social withdrawal. In the field of gerontology there is a growing body of scholarship aimed at critiquing covert ideological presuppositions about aging and later life. This includes assessments of research approaches which actually produce negative images of aging as they inadvertently reinforce the "failure model" of aging, a preoccupation with dependency and decline in old age (Manheimer, 1990).

Gerontology (the science of aging) and andragogy (an awkward term for the study of adult learning processes) seem to be on vastly different courses. The scientific study of aging is dominated by clinical concerns related to aging as a process of irreversible decline. Gerontology research is heavily invested in seeing aging as a problem. Older adult education takes as its point of departure the strengths and developmental possibilities of later life. While there are certainly points of intersection between studying aging and studying learning in retirement, most older adults shun the study of gerontology since it largely ignores healthy and productive older people.

If, for women, education means reevaluation of self and gender, as well as a ticket to participation in the economy, does older adult education have similar meanings? The change in attitudes toward older people has come more from the leadership of aging organizations such as AARP, NCOA, and the Gray Panthers than from universities or their research institutes. But the upsurge in opportunities for older learners, at least in the U.S., does indicate a breakthrough in changing the self-images of older persons. Growing numbers of physically fit, mobile, moderately to well-educated, middle-class retirees are seeking the chance to discover worlds of knowledge, culture, information and self-reflection, along with like-minded peers. On the pragmatic side, some university-based programs are providing retraining and certification for new careers for older adults. The University of Massachusetts at Boston offers gerontological training to senior citizens seeking employment as practitioners in the field. It is likely that more such vocational programs will be offered.

What is useful about the parallel between changing images of adults who are older and women in general is how, for both, new roles and capabilities seem as natural as were the prejudices previously held. Where the parallel falls short is the unchanging fact that later life does bring limits to activity and, eventually, frailty and death. There is a danger here of overlooking or denying this fact—of superimposing yet another stereotype of the ideal senior as perpetually healthy and active right up to the moment of death (Cole, 1988).

However the phenomenon of the older learner is explained, the originating sources do not necessarily determine the direction of either development or fruition. A rationale for long-term higher education support for older learners needs critical attention. If the chief rationale for college-based programs is the argument that they too are taxpayers, and therefore deserve access to higher education, then older adult education will run headlong into society's commitment to higher education as the right of the young as future productive members of society. While this might not be a conflict today, eventually when the economy dips and budget cuts must be made the attitude may well change. Then, unless a learning-in-retirement program has proved to be significantly valuable to undergraduates and faculty members, and/or is entirely self-sufficient, it is likely that the program will be among the first to be eliminated.

Market demand and fee-driven educational programs responding to consumer demands from older adults will need to deepen their philosophical foundations, or else the elder students will be regarded (at worst) as a special-interest group in competition with younger age groups for campus resources, or (at best) as simply superfluous to currents of educational and social change. What is needed is a comprehensive view of older adult education that identifies the older person's significant place in the development continuum, and regards that person as an important contributing member of a college or university community.

Can the institutional foundation for third-age learners be erected upon a moral imperative asserting that it is the obligation of older people to act in such a way that their concerns and contributions serve both to secure positive meanings for life's third quarter and to help to improve the lives of those of other generations? This philosophical presupposition undergirds the programs of the NCCCR and is supported by the initial responses of seniors in the center's (albeit short) history.

10

Coasting Home!

MILTON R. STERN

"I was a hard student until I entered on the business of life, the duties of which leave no idle time to those disposed to fulfil them; and now, retired, and at the age of seventy-six, I am again a hard student."—Thomas Jefferson, letter to Dr. Vine Utley, 21 March 1819; The Oxford Book of Ages. *Oxford University Press New York 1985.*

Dr. Manheimer's preceding chapter has a quality that challenged me to address in this summary the meaning of *all* the activity described earlier—a formidable undertaking. I write as both a long-time supporter and believer in LIRs, and a newly retired (1991) continuing educator. Thus, I will use the first person plural in both senses: *We* are retired older adults, and *we* are committed to lifelong learning.

The title of this chapter arises from personal experience. In 1949 my then nuclear family—wife, one-year-old daughter, and I—summered on Martha's Vineyard, in a white clapboard cottage rented from a Gay Head Indian, Mr. Lorenzo Jeffers. We had a lovely situation: The house folded into a slope with low, windswept bushes, and through a "V" in the hills we could just see Buzzards Bay and, on clear nights, twinkling 20 miles away, the lights of New Bedford. The house was small but compact, with wild roses all around. There was a boulder in front, on a scrubby lawn where Debbie, my daughter, played in the summer sunshine with our two Siamese cats. The cottage had no inside plumbing or electricity. Water came from a pump in a zinc sink in the kitchen. But the place did have a luxury for such a cottage, a kerosene-powered refrigerator. All in all, an idyll—particularly when you consider that a three-month rental was just $400.

I remember one sunny August morning in the small dining room, seeing my daughter, who had just emerged from the crawling stage to first, tentative steps, squatting next to the bookshelves in the corner, chewing on a book. The shelves were full of the period's typical summer-house accumulation (you know: *The Boy Allies in the Balkans,* and *Tom Swift and His Electric Runabout* for the boys; *Anne of Green Gables* for the girls; with Paul Leicester Ford and oh-so-darling Elinor Glyn for adults), all in those unjacketed, figured-cloth, dark green or red or yellow covers of the late nineties or early years of this century. But is seemed to me Debbie was gnawing on an untypical volume, and I was intrigued by that. Of course, my first thoughts were "I don't want her to get ill," and "I don't want her to eat our landlord's property." After all, we were renting. When I took the book away from her she cried briefly, but was soon distracted by something more edible, *The Rover Boys at School.* By then, however, I had become absorbed in what she has been chewing. It was the leather-bound log of a whaling vessel, the good ship *Mary,* out of New Bedford in 1839 and back in 1843. A four-year voyage!

Call me Ishmael? Remember, we were in Gay Head: Shades of *Moby-Dick,* of Ahab, Tashtego, and QueeQueg! Our neighbor in the house just beyond view over the winding, grassy track was Mr. Jeffers' cousin, Amos Smalley, 76 years old in 1949, who as a crew member on a whaling vessel in 1902 had *indeed* harpooned a white whale. This incident was described in detail in the tattered New Bedford newspaper that he allowed me to read. And naturally, in those days before the now ubiquitous concerns about endangered species, the romance of whaling, illustrated by Rockwell Kent's block prints for *Moby Dick,* was much in my head.

I spent bemused hours going over the log of the whaler *Mary.* It was a laconic narrative: Most days, the captain entered only latitude, longitude, and one-line comments about the weather. When there was a notable event he reported it matter-of-factly, with no emphasis. The ship's cook deserted in Madagascar; the second mate and two hands were lost when a whale crushed their boat with a blow from its tail. When the crew killed a whale the log showed one horizontally by means of a little (wood block?) stamped impression. And if the whale was lost, the captain used the stamp vertically, head down. As I recall, he had different stamps for sperm whales, right whales, and bowhead whales. But I'm not certain about that particular point.

I *am* still acutely aware, however, that the log went on week after week, month after month, and year after year, as the voyage went on and on—like a life. Finally they had filled their barrels with whale oil, and from the Indian Ocean the *Mary* turned back, around the Cape of Good Hope, through the South Atlantic, the Doldrums, the raging storms—all with no editorial comment by the captain until at last there was the entry at the top of a left-hand page: "Off Florida" and (underlined three times) "Coasting Home!" How marvelous! I had not until a few years ago, thinking of my own retirement, considered "Coasting Home!" save literally as the feelings of a man far away from us in time. Now? Let me not labor the metaphor, but in our age group, whether we be believers or what you will, we are all coasting home. There may be storms off Hatteras, but there will be home port for all of us.

Intriguing, the years that remain: What do we keep or throw away; what do we *do*? What role do LIRs play in the penultimate part of the voyage? What issues should be of active concern to those who lead LIRs or have an institutional responsibility for them? We need techniques to help us to explore the unfamiliar—or perhaps, more to the point, to help us to feel the newly strange shape and outline of the familiar. Do we respond in the same way we did years ago to the stirring nineteenth-century declaration of Tennyson's *Ulysses,* "We are what we are"?

Speaking for myself, now in my seventies, I find more modest, reflective sense in the words of Satchel Paige: "The past is a long and twisty road." One responds, of course ("resonates" is the chic, up-to-date word), to "the great Achilles whom we knew," and "Far on the ringing plains of windy Troy," and the poem's booming surf—how could one fail to hear it even now? But perhaps Tennyson was more deviously professional and aware of audience than we know. He was only 33 when he wrote *Ulysses*. On the other hand, he wrote *Crossing the Bar* at 89, and although it has a more mellow feel, it is no more serenely assured than *Ulysses* of what is to come. Were High Victorians of whatever age still full of Romantic Youth, Matthew Arnold's *Dover Beach* to the contrary notwithstanding? Whatever the case, then, today we are dealing with an ever larger group of older people who represent opportunity to themselves and to universities, and must be considered in the context of our own times.

LIRs Belong to Their Members

The question of organization, as discussed in earlier chapters, remains an arguable one. I tend to come down on the side of nondirective administrative attitudes on the part of universities, and this extends to curriculum development as well. By "nondirective" I do not mean "noninvolved." But I think the lines between involvement, persuasive advice, and institutional control are delicate indeed. To do well by the newly discovered older members of the university requires careful consideration of the issues and problems discussed in earlier chapters. Still, there is no one ideal structure suitable for all institutions or for all groups of retirees. Older people, like all other adults (and perhaps even more than most), vote with their feet when they feel slighted by programs established for them. The central requisite of curricula development for LIRs should be the involvement of the learners in planning. If that is done, *and attention is paid,* then even the most rigidly structured organization may rightly claim to have responded to the needs of the students. And the members of the ever-increasing, varied LIRs will make insistent demands that programs be right for *them.*

There is no place for dogma in the education of students of the Third Age. Of course, one cannot speak for the needs and wants of all men and women, but one may extract certain generalities from one's own experiences. In doing so, it is wise to be somewhat diffident about sweeping conclusions. Thus, to what extent will the current stereotype of retired people be replicated by the stereotype of people now in their forties, the Baby Boom generation? Will the Baby Boomers maintain cohort characteristics as they grow older? Even in the sixties, their formative decade, did they have a distinguishing pervasive outlook? Does a public cultural identity of a generation conquer curmudgeonly individualism? Probably not, but how many exceptions are there? Most of us, even as we grow older and "become more so," tend to agree with and accept cultural definitions of who we are.

To what extent is "lifestyle" an invention of media and promotional wordsmiths? Do older people put on the mask they are expected to wear— and, if so, to what extent are they (behind the mask) substantially different from the stereotype, or from each other as individuals? Is it possible that some of what being old means is a passively acquired characteristic, a necessary social device of younger people as they seek to make society more manageable? It simply takes too much time to treat everyone as an individual. Henry Thoreau had to retreat from Concord (a crowded place, he thought) to Walden Pond because it was crucial to him to treat others as he would be treated—as an individual. If everyone is shaped by the culture, then do older people need ways to live as a separate group, to retreat to their own "Walden Ponds"?

Older people who cling to their youth are frequently thought to be somewhat comic or pathetic, and surely behaving inappropriately. So one expects that the BBs (Baby Boomers) will preserve certain characteristics which will be thought inappropriate by their grandchildren 20 years hence. Or will they? Will there be a paradigm shift as an aging population shapes social mores and attitudes in ways unforeseen today, ways more to its liking? Majorities have more than political clout: Majorities can shape society.

Whatever the case, LIRs are here to stay as part of higher education. They are a natural outcome of the growth of continuing education for people in their middle years. In the mid-sixties I urged a revised definition of middle age (at least in developed countries) to include people from 35 to 65. I was correct about the upper edge but wrong about the lower, since to be 35 in 1991 was still to be young. Middle age these days doesn't begin until around 50, with allowance of course for diet, genetic endowment, lifestyle, and degree of consumption of abusive substances.

So we come to the kind of life that older people will be living in the next century. LIRs are a phenomenon, a bridge to a future that will have a preponderantly older population. It remains to be seen what changes of attitude will take place among older adults and college administrators. But for now, the LIRs represent a significant positive environment for older Americans—if, that is, the organization is not in the hands of others. By that I mean younger professionals under the command of university administrators who have many other things (deficits, faculty unions, tenure fights, campus activism) on their minds. Under such leadership, carefully calibrated doses of specific learning may be prescribed precisely when a more holistic approach would be much healthier.

I would not deny the value of generational interaction in the intergenerational classroom. Both younger and older students should gain. But that is not the be-all and end-all of higher education's policy concerns for its aged constituency. Just as young people need an identity, so do older students. Here, passed on from Dr. Cecilia Zissis, Associate Dean of Students Emerita of Purdue University, is an anonymously authored descriptive checklist—entertaining, illuminating, and all too accurate.

Ways in Which You Can Tell You Are an Older Student

- You are the only person sitting in the front row of the class.
- The music in the student union gives you a headache.
- You remember when John F. Kennedy [Herbert Hoover—MRS] was president.
- You think the legal drinking age should be raised to 30.
- You get nauseated watching a freshman eating a twinkie and a Coke for breakfast.
- You have never played a video game.
- Your favorite shoes are older than your classmates. [Not their shoes, mind you, but them!—MRS]
- Someone tells you he didn't think there was life after 40.
- You don't carry your books in a backpack.
- You talk about painting the living room over spring break while everyone else is talking about Florida.
- You suspect that the girl sitting next to you paid more for her jeans than you did for your first car.
- You are the first one to arrive in class, and the last one to leave.
- You go to bed thankful that you will never be 18 again.

There's wisdom for you, but implicit in the list also is the sense of *difference*. The intergenerational classroom is a fine innovation, but that's just one part of being an older student—*or* a younger one. Both groups need a retreat, a place of their own. And I say "group" because in spite of the fact that we all have individual differences, we all are acculturated *as* groups. Some of what we do cuts across age levels: An older adult can play chess or checkers or gin rummy with ten-year-olds, or study in class with students of almost any school level after (let's say) ninth grade. But youngsters have an age cohort with which to identify. Older people need the same kind of group identity—and LIRs provide that sanctuary.

For there to be intergenerational communication we must either discover or create a kind of Rosetta Stone. In considerable part the intergenerational classroom can provide such two-way translation, because different subcultures (of different ages) have their own ways of seeing and behaving. So, like all other groups in our multicultural society, older men and women want to belong both to the larger group and to their own smaller group. (Even Thoreau visited Concord when he got lonely.) Like everybody else, they want it all—but of course will have to settle for less.

LIRs, then, are an excellent way to gain that fulfillment of self that cannot be achieved by living entirely in the larger society. On the other side, LIRs can represent an agglomeration of individuals whose effect is greater than their numbers suggest. They affirm the importance of interaction in learning. Education is a social transaction, incomplete without other people; education may not require a teacher, but it surely requires other students, other learners. LIRs are in the process of becoming an institution (or at least a social entity) of consequence, as valuable in its way as church or club or family.

LIRs satisfy a basic human need. When we say that learning never ends we are not merely uttering a fervent wish or a persuasive marketing slogan, but rather speaking about a human trait—the need to learn—that has always been, and will remain, necessary to life itself. Someone once said that our dread of death is partially based upon our insatiable curiosity: We simply cannot bear not knowing what will happen tomorrow. Or the thought of never learning anything new. Those of us who are believers are sure that we will somehow continue after we die, but then those of us who aren't disagree. In this respect a real-life exchange of hypothetical opinions sounds remarkably like many another exchange in any given LIR class session. However, in this case we all shall find out sooner or later who is right.

For older men and women, LIRs support the human need to learn. They are life-enhancing organizations that will endure. What do we mean by "learning in retirement"? We do not mean simply the elementary satisfaction of finding out some fact or other, but rather more complex processes—surrounding an idea with understanding, or letting an idea surround us. Both of these processes were present when we were young. So what do we mean by learning at this later stage? Is learning only a tool, at (say) age 70? Sometimes yes, if we want to catch up with some useful technology; learning to use a computer is an obvious example. With some exceptions, learning has been obviously tool-oriented in terms of the socialized direction that education has taken for the past hundred years in America. Is that in the process of change? People now over 70 are not newly hatched and needing to be imprinted; they have had a much deeper experience than young people, even those in their forties. Learning for them is a way of life, a way to better confront life's persistent complexities. While it is interesting, and even useful, to talk about mutual education between generations, it is even more important to realize that older people constitute a *special* subculture. They themselves know that to be so, and it behooves those in universities who relate to them to get the message.

The Uses of the Past

We older people live under two flags, in another country as well as our own. The past is that other country, and we have to be able, and be enabled, to explore and explain its richness if we are to help ourselves and continue to contribute to the future of our children and theirs. While to our children our past is history, to us it still is part of our life. And we are its only interpreters. That is our peculiar role in the larger society.

We need the social experience of our own peer groups to articulate our experience. We really haven't lived life fully until we have examined it and explored it for ourselves and among ourselves. This, then, is what our retirement programs have as an overarching function of our work together: to share that experience—to share our generation's history, our mutual biography. The future should record not only all of our children's history, but our own as well, and the continuity that we can provide will only enhance that future as well as that record.

LIRs are not only for ourselves, but for our society as well. They function within the framework of that long-lived institution, the university, which has a history that goes back a thousand years and more. Early in the 1960s, in *The City in History,* Lewis Mumford pointed out that:

> With its long memory, its vital international affiliations, its disciplined devotion to intellectual communication and cooperation, the university has become the central nucleus in the new urban and cultural grid.

With uneven pace, the university as a social institution seeks to live up to that assignment, an assignment that includes higher education's responsibility to the older generation. For their part, LIRs represent a return to the human role as against the overspecialization and disciplinary rigidities of academe, and this is sure to have a more profound effect than we can imagine at this moment. This new ingredient, this "yeast," will help shape the universities of the future. LIRs, these new Waldens of individualism and differentiation, are important to educated older people; but they may be even more valuable and instructive to those who come after us, and to their societies.

Coasting home, then, is not a downhill slide. It is not a jettisoning of responsibility or a casting-off of lines that tie us to the larger society. Quite the opposite. It is the most promising and satisfying chapter of a long and bountiful voyage—a voyage of discovery, rich with harvest.

Appendixes

I

Learning-in-Retirement Bylaws

Article I: Names, Offices

Section 1. Name. The Name of the organization shall be (_____).

Section 2. Offices. The office of the LIR shall be in (location).

Article II: Purpose

The LIR provides opportunities for intellectual and cultural stimulation and growth for people of retirement age. It offers opportunities to explore a virtually limitless array of topics, such as science, art, language and society that one may not have been able to study previously.

Learning occurs in a pleasant social atmosphere in classes with, and taught by, one's peers. The instructors are not paid, and they must be members of the LIR. Sharing their interest and expertise with the class can give the instructors personal satisfaction and new dimensions to the understanding of their subjects.

Modeled from the LAMP Program, University of Texas at Austin

Article III: Memberships and Dues

Section 1. Categories of members. The LIR shall have such categories of membership as determined by the LIR Council (see Article V describing LIR Council) and approved by the voting members of the LIR.

Section 2. Assessment of Dues. The Dues structure for the LIR shall be determined by the LIR Council. Any changes shall be approved by the voting membership of the LIR.

Section 3. Compensation. Members shall not receive compensation or reimbursement for their services.

Article IV: Meetings

Section 1. Regular and Special. The full membership of the LIR shall meet at least twice each calendar year. One such meeting shall be the annual business meeting of the LIR. Special meetings shall be called as necessary by the Council. Meetings of the LIR shall be at times and locations designated by the Council. The membership shall be notified of the time, location, and purpose of any meeting at least thirty days prior to the meeting.

Section 2. Quorum. A quorum for a meeting of the LIR membership shall be 30 percent of the membership or their proxies present and voting.

Section 3. Proxies. A member may designate a proxy to represent him/her, if done so in writing to the LIR Coordinator prior to the annual business meeting of the LIR.

Section 4. Mail Ballot. Voting on all matters which may be properly considered by a meeting of the LIR may be conducted by mail, with the exception of amendments to the bylaws.

Section 5. Sub-Units. Sub-units meetings such as Committee meetings shall be held at times and places convenient to the sub-unit members, except that sub-unit meetings shall not conflict with the regular meeting of the LIR.

Section 6. Minutes. Minutes of meetings of the General Membership shall be kept and constitute a record of the business conducted by the General Membership.

Article V: LIR Council

Section 1. General Powers. The LIR Council shall supervise, control and direct the affairs of the LIR, pursue its purposes, and determine its policies, consistent with and subject to policies of the University, except as otherwise provided in the Charter of the LIR or these Bylaws. Consistent with the general powers, the Council may adopt such operating rules, policies, and procedures as necessary.

Section 2. Composition. The composition of the LIR Council shall be determined by the membership of the LIR. University Coordinator shall serve without vote.

Section 3. Officers. The officers of the LIR shall be the officers of the Council.

Section 4. Meetings. The Council shall meet in each calendar year. Meetings of the Council shall be at times and locations designated by the Council. Council members shall be notified of the time, location, and purpose of any meeting at least fifteen days prior to the meeting, unless a special meeting is called.

Section 5. Quorum. A quorum shall be fifty-one percent (51%) of the membership of the Council entitled to vote, present and voting at a meeting of the Council.

Section 6. Mail Ballot. Voting on all matters which may be properly considered by the Council at a meeting may be conducted by mail.

Section 7. Minutes. Minutes of meetings of the Council shall be kept and constitute a record of the business conducted by the Council.

Section 8. Replacement. A council Member may resign at any time by giving written notice to the elected head of the LIR. Such resignation shall take effect at the time specified therein or, if no time is specified, at the time of acceptance thereof as determined by the elected head of the LIR. A Council member absent from meetings of the Council without excuse may be removed by majority vote of the Directors at a regular or special meeting at which a quorum is present. Vacancies that may occur on the Council by reason of death, resignation, removal, or otherwise, shall be filled by the action of the remaining members of the Council.

Article VI: Officers

Section 1. Officers. The officers of the LIR, their qualifications, and their duties shall be determined or modified by the membership of the LIR. The current officers of the LIR and the duties of such officers shall be listed in the Policies and Procedures Manual of the LIR. All officers serve until their successors have been duly elected and assume office.

Article VII: Administration

Section 1. UNIVERSITY COORDINATOR. The University shall employ a Coordinator to act as a liaison between the University, its sub-units and the LIR and carry out administrative work for the LIR. The University shall fix by contract and/or performance plans, the duties, responsibilities, and compensation of this position.

Section 2. The University shall appoint all professional and support staff.

Section 3. Fund Raising. The Council shall have the power to raise funds, and receive gifts or other assets on behalf of the LIR for purposes of advancing the LIR. All fund raising activities must be coordinated with the University Development Office.

Section 4. Procedures. *Roberts Rules' of Order, Revised* shall govern all meetings of the Council and the LIR, insofar as they are not inconsistent with these Bylaws, unless other specific procedures are provided by the Council.

Article VIII: Committees

Section 1. Committees. The elected head of the LIR with the approval of the LIR Council shall establish and dissolve the standing and special committees of the LIR.

Section 2. Mail Ballots. Voting on all matters which may be properly considered at a meeting of the committee may be conducted by mail.

Article IX: Finances

Section 1. Banking. The funds of the LIR shall be deposited in such financial institutions as may be approved by the University following procedures established by the University.

Section 2. Fiscal Year. The fiscal year of the LIR shall be the same as that of the University.

Section 3. Budget. The LIR shall operate under a budget recommended annually by the LIR Council, reported to the membership at the annual business meeting of the LIR, and approved by the University.

Section 4. Audit. The finances of the LIR shall be audited and reported by the University.

Article X: Dissolution

The LIR may be dissolved or merged with another similar corporation conducting substantially the same activities, upon approval of a plan of dissolution adopted by a two-thirds vote of the total membership of the Council and a majority of the voting of the membership of the LIR and approved by the University.

Article XI: Amendments

Amendments to these Bylaws may be proposed by any member of the LIR. Such proposals shall be referred to a Charter/Bylaws review group for study and recommendation to the Council. If approved by the Council, the recommended amendment will be distributed to the membership at least thirty (30) days prior to a regular meeting. Amendments shall be adopted by majority vote of the voting members.

II

Sample Membership Information Form

The information on this form helps us in planning for our members and is for internal use only.

Today's Date _____

Name _____ Sex _____ Birthdate _____

By what first name do you wish to be called? _____

Address _____
          Street   City   ZIP

Name of neighborhood or subdivision, if any _____

Telephone _____ Marital Status ____ M ____ S

Schools attended _____

Field of study _____ Degrees _____

Occupation (now and/or before retirement) _____

_____

_____

II. Sample Membership Information Form

When did you move to the area? _____

Where did you live before? _____

Do you have suggestions for future classes? _____

_____

_____

Many of our members have enjoyed teaching a group of adults or coordinating a study group. Might this interest you? _____ What subject areas would interest you most? _____

How did you learn about this program? _____

In case of emergency, please contact _____

_____

III

Program Survey

In the Spring of 1989, the National University Continuing Education Association sponsored a survey of all institutions of higher education in the United States to gather information on programs they were offering for older adults. Of the 3,300 surveys mailed, 580 responses were returned with 380 institutions indicating they had special programs for older adults.

TYPE OF PROGRAM

Most of the programs are academically oriented and a large proportion of universities offer reduced or free tuition to their regular college courses. A few programs focus on special interests such as social activities only, medical support, or travel.

ACADEMIC HOME

For those programs affiliated with colleges or universities, the most common academic home was the college of continuing education. About 25 percent were supported by an academic college or unit other than continuing education and about 1 percent were located in the university relations office.

FINANCIAL MATTERS

Most programs reported they are self-supporting. The mean annual operating budget, exclusive of staff costs, was $16,200. The mean annual membership fee was $255.

Most offer some form of scholarship aid, with an average award of $255. Most scholarship recipients are selected through a formal process, with about one-half using a committee. Scholarships are funded by member donations, waiver of fees, or university subsidies, and some are budgeted from operating revenues, so all members pay a portion of the scholarship aid.

Seventy-five percent of the programs conduct fund-raising by the members but only 35 percent of the programs list fund-raising as an activity sanctioned by the host college or university.

Seventy-five percent of the programs indicate a portion of the members' dues are considered tax-deductible.

STAFF

Approximately 90 percent of the programs have paid professional and support staff. The mean number of paid staff is five, with most programs reporting (the mode) only one staff member.

Volunteer staff perform a variety of functions, including administrative/clerical, curriculum, registration, marketing, hospitality, and travel. The average size of the volunteer group ranges from four to 13 per category.

MEMBERSHIP

The vast majority of programs establish a minimum age requirement, with 57 as the average minimum age reported. The most frequently occurring age minimum (the mode) is 65.

The average yearly attrition rate (defined as the percentage of members who fail to renew membership each year) is 32 percent.

Most programs limit the size of membership. The average size is 137.

The average participation rate in classes is 80 percent, with most reporting a 100 percent rate.

Two-thirds of the programs require some formal application for membership. Only a few require their members to have a minimum educational level or professional status, or actually be retired.

RECRUITMENT

The most common and most effective recruitment strategy reported was "word of mouth." Direct mailing of brochures was second, followed by distributing a catalog, news stories, and free media (public service announcements). Slide or video presentations were the least used and paid advertising was the least effective.

LEADERS WITHIN THE MEMBERSHIP

Membership in programs for older adults can include people with strong leadership backgrounds or careers of prominence. The most common category of member/leader was "professional," followed by "community leader," "university faculty," "business executive," "political leader," "labor leader," and finally "university trustee."

NEW PROGRAM STARTS

The trend displayed in the graph in Figure AIII.1 shows that the number of new programs is increasing. These programs are on the leading edge of the age wave of older adults that will continue to rise into the next century. These programs are pioneering efforts to meet an ever-increasing demand for continuing intellectual stimulation for older adults.

Figure AIII.1 **Number of New Programs for Older Adults 1954–1988**

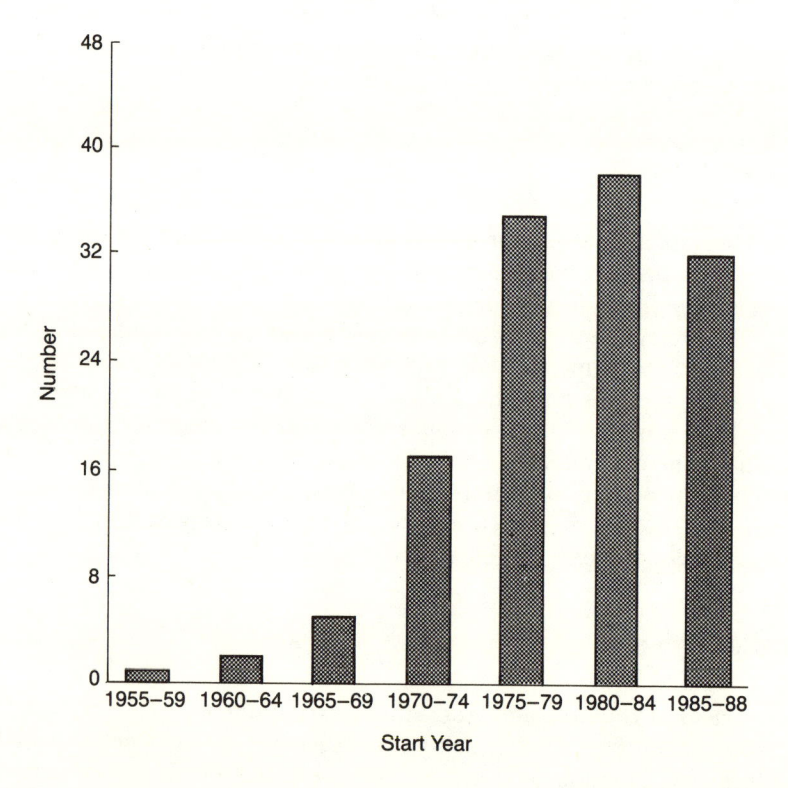

IV

Higher Education Institutions Sponsoring Member-Driven LIR-Type Programs

If you have an LIR-type program and it is not listed below, please contact Dr. Richard B. Fischer, University of Delaware, Division of Continuing Education, Newark, DE 19716.

    Aims Community College (Learning Throughout Life)

    Albertus Magnus College (Institute for Learning in Retirement)*

    American University (Institute for Learning in Retirement)‡

    Amherst College (Five College Learning in Retirement Institute)*

    Anne Arundel Community College (Learning Institute for Elders)‡

    Appalachian State University (Institute for Senior Scholars)‡

    Aquinas College (Emeritus College)

---

*Member, Elderhostel Institute Network
†Member, Association of Learning in Retirement Organizations, West
‡Member, National University Continuing Education Association

Arapahoe Community College (Emeritus College)

Asnuntuck Community College (University of the Third Age)*

Auburn University (Academy of Lifelong Learning)*‡

Austin Community College (Lifetime Learning Institute)

Beaver College (Community Scholars)

Bluffton College (Institute for Learning in Retirement)*

Boston University (Evergreen)‡

Brazosport College (Adult Life and Learning Program)

Brooklyn College (Institute for Retired Professionals and Executives)*

Brown University (Community for Learning in Retirement)

Burlington County College (Learning Institute for Elders)*

California State University–Bakersfield (Sixty-Plus)*†

California State University–Chico (Eldercollege)*†‡

California State University–Fullerton (Continuing Learning Experience Institute)†‡

California State University–Northridge (Sage Society)*†‡

California State University–Sacramento (Renaissance Society)*†‡

Cape Cod Community College (Academy for Lifelong Learning)*

Case Western Reserve University (Senior Scholars Program)

Cedar Crest College (Institute for Learning in Retirement)

Centenary College (Senior Adult Education Program)

Central Connecticut State University

Christopher Newport College (Elder Learning Society)*

Clark College (Focus on Mature Learning)

College of Boca Raton (Dimensions for Life)*

College of DuPage (Older Adult Institute)

College of Mount St. Vincent (College Emeritus)

College of Notre Dame of Maryland (Renaissance Institute)*

College of San Mateo (Emeritus College)

Columbia Greene Community College (Adult Learning Institute)*

IV. LIR-Type Programs

Cornell College (Chautauqua Program for Senior Adults)

Cowley County Community College (Institute for Lifetime Learning)*

Curry College (Seniors for Lifelong Learning)

Cuyahoga Community College (Elders Program)

Delaware Valley College (Center for Learning in Retirement)

Del Mar College

Dixie College (Institute of Continued Learning)*

Duke University (Institute for Learning in Retirement)*‡

Eckerd College (Academy of Senior Professionals)*‡

El Paso Community College (Senior Adult Program)

Endicott College (Center for Creative Aging)*

Emory University (Emory Senior University)

Fairfield University (Institute for Retired Professionals)

Fairleigh Dickinson University (Educational Program for Older Adults)

Felician College (Senior Adult Program)

Florida International University (Elders Institute)‡

Fordham University (The College at 60)

George Brown College–Canada (Seniors Association)

George Mason University (Adult Education Center)*‡

Glendale Community College (Emeritus College)

Grant MacEwan Community College–Canada (Senior Studies Institute)

Hampshire College (Five College Learning in Retirement Institute)*

Hartford Consortium for Higher Education (Adult Learning Program)*

Harvard University (Institute for Learning in Retirement)*‡

Hofstra University (Professionals and Executives in Retirement)

Hope College (Academy of Senior Professionals)*

Johns Hopkins University (Evergreen Society)‡

Johnson County Community College (Lifetime Learning Institute)‡

Kingsborough Community College (My Turn)

Lakeland Community College (Elder Institute)

Lee College (Senior Adult Institute)

Long Island University (Center for Creative Retirement

Loyola College of Maryland (Creative Living)‡

Manatee Junior College (Retired Executives and Professionals)

Mars Hill College (Learning Institute for Elders)

Maryland Community College (Lifelong Learning in Maryland)*

McGill University–Canada (Institute for Learning in Retirement)*

Modesto Junior College (Institute of Continued Learning)†

Monterey Peninsula College (Gentrain Society)†

Mount Holyoke College (Five College Learning in Retirement Institute)*

Muhlenberg College (Institute for Learning in Retirement)

Neosho County Community College (Continued Lifetime Learning)

New England College (Learning Institute)*‡

New School for Social Research (Institute for Retired Professionals)*

North Carolina State University (Encore)*‡

Northampton County Community College (Late Start Program)

Northern Essex Community College (Life-Long Learning Program)

Northwest Technical College (Center for Lifelong Learning)*

Northwestern University (Institute for Learning in Retirement)*

Nova University (Institute for Retired Professionals)*‡

Oakland Community College

Ohio State University–Lima (Institute for Learning in Retirement)*‡

Pace University (Pace Active Retirement Center)

Palm Beach Junior College (Institute of New Dimensions)

Parkland College (Lifelong Learners Club)

Pensacola Junior College (Seniors Club)

Pima County Community College (Senior Education Program)

Rio Salado Community College (Institute for Retired Professionals)

Roanoke College (Elderscholar)

Rochester Institute of Technology (Athenaeum)‡

IV. LIR-Type Programs

Rockland Community College (Institute for Senior Education)

Ryerson Polytechnical Institute–Canada (Seniors Studies)

Salisbury State College (Institute for Retired Professionals)

San Diego State University–Rancho Bernardo†

San Diego State University–San Diego (Educational Growth Opportunity)†‡

San Francisco State University (Sixty Plus)†‡

Skidmore College (Studies for Mature Adults)

Smith College (Five College Learning in Retirement Institute)*

Southern Illinois University–Edwardsville (Metro-East Institute of Lifetime Learning)‡

Spokane Falls Community College (Institute for Extended Learning)

Springfield College (Institute in Later Life)*

St. Joseph College (Senior Academy)‡

St. Michael's College (Elder Education Enrichment)*

St. Xavier College (Renaissance Academy)*‡

State University of New York–Binghamton (LYCEUM)*‡

State University of New York–Stony Brook (The Round Table)‡

Syracuse University (Institute for Retired Professionals)‡

Temple University (Association for Retired Professionals)‡

Texas Tech University (Lifespan Learning Institute)*‡

Union College (Academy of Lifelong Learning)*‡

University of Alabama (New Horizons)*‡

University of Arizona (Seniors' Achievement and Growth Through Education Society)†‡

University of California–Berkeley (Center for Learning in Retirement)*†‡

University of California–Los Angeles (Plato Society)*†‡

University of California–San Diego (Institute for Continued Learning)*†‡

University of California–Santa Cruz (Lifelong Learners)*†

University of Central Florida (Learning Institute for Elders)*‡

University of Cincinnati (Institute for Learning in Retirement)*‡

University of Connecticut*‡

University of Delaware (Academy of Lifelong Learning)‡

University of Hawaii–Hilo (Hawaii Island Senior Institute)*

University of Lowell (Learning in Retirement Association)*‡

University of Massachusetts (Five College Learning in Retirement Institute)*‡

University of Miami (FL) (Institute for Retired Professionals)*‡

University of Michigan (Learning in Retirement Program)*‡

University of Minnesota (University for Seniors)*‡

University of Nevada–Reno (Elder College)*‡

University of Nevada–Las Vegas (Excell)‡

University of New Hampshire (Active Retirement Association)*‡

University of New Mexico (Learning Institute for Elders)*‡

University of New Orleans‡

University of North Carolina–Asheville (North Carolina Center for Creative Retirement)‡

University of North Carolina–Chapel Hill (Village Elders)‡

University of Oklahoma (Academy of Retired Professionals)‡

University of Pennsylvania (Senior Associate Program)‡

University of Regina–Canada (Seniors' Education Centre)*

University of San Francisco (Fromm Institute for Lifelong Learning)†

University of South Carolina–Aiken (Academy for Lifelong Learning)*‡

University of South Carolina–Coastal Carolina College (Third Quarter)*‡

University of Southern Maine (New Dimensions)

University of Strathclyde–Scotland (Learning-in-Later Life Association)

University of Texas–Austin (Learning Activities for Mature Persons)‡

University of Texas–El Paso (Center for Lifelong Learning)*

University of Texas–San Antonio (Academy of Learning in Retirement)

University of West Florida (Center for Lifelong Learning)*

University of Wisconsin–Madison (Plato Society)‡

IV. LIR-Type Programs

University of Wisconsin–Milwaukee (Guild for Learning in Retirement)*‡

University of Wisconsin–River Falls (Senior Outreach Studies)

University of Wyoming (Laramie Senior Lysium)‡

Valencia Community College (Institute of Lifetime Learning)

Virginia Polytechnic Institute (New Dimensions)‡

Virginia Commonwealth University (Free University for Senior Citizens)‡

Westchester Community College (Retirement Institute)

Wilson College (Institute for Retired Persons)

Young Harris College (Institute for Continuing Learning)*

V

Sample First-Year Annual LIR Budget

Expenses

I. Direct Costs
    Personnel
        Program Coordinator $6,300.00
        Secretary   2,200.00
            Subtotal $8,500.00
    Travel
        Program Coordinator   300.00
            Subtotal   300.00
    Supplies and Expenses
        Office Supplies   150.00
        Audio-Visual Aids   250.00
        Films and Slides   250.00
        Photocopying Services   50.00
        Office Furniture   1,000.00
        Photography   100.00
        Postage   250.00
        Telephones   600.00
        Copy Machine Rental   200.00
        Coffee Supplies   400.00
            Subtotal   4,250.00

V. Sample First-Year Annual LIR Budget

Occupancy
　Classroom Space　　　　　　　　　　　　　1,920.00
　($12.00 per one-and-a-half hour session ×
　4 sessions/week × 40 weeks)
　　　　　Subtotal　　　　　　　　　　　　　　　　　　　1,920.00

Promotion
　Brochure (3-color, 6 × 9, 10,000)　　　1,000.00
　Posters (3-color, 15 × 24, 500)　　　　　 300.00
　Newspaper Advertising　　　　　　　　　 1,200.00
　　　　　Subtotal　　　　　　　　　　　　　　　　　　　2,500.00

II.　Indirect Costs or University Overhead　　　　　1,500.00
　　　　　　　　　　GRAND TOTAL　　　　　　　$18,970.00

Income

Annual Membership Fees
　100 members @ $175.00　　　　　$17,500.00
　　　　　　　Subtotal　　　　　　　　　　　　　　　$17,500.00
　　　　　　　GRAND TOTAL　　　　　　　　　$17,500.00

NOTE: Sample of cost categories. Dollar amounts presented for illustrative purposes only.

VI

Memorandum of Understanding Concerning LIR Operations (Supplement to Bylaws)

The purpose of this memorandum is to describe the procedures that, under the rules and regulations of The University of _____ and the Division of Continuing Education, must be followed in administering the LIR program.

LIR is a program of _____, Division of Continuing Education of the University of _____, which was developed in accord with a mission to provide continuing education opportunities in professional development and personal enrichment.

Participation in the LIR program is offered through payment of membership dues. Membership is offered to any individual 55 years old or older. Membership in the program entitles one to attend its educational and social activities.

RECEIPTS PAYABLE TO UNIVERSITY

All revenue generated by the LIR program must be deposited in accounts maintained by the University for the Division of Continuing Education. Checks written to the LIR program must therefore be made payable to The University of _____. All checks and cash should be promptly turned over to the Business Office for deposit with the University.

EXPENDITURES

University procedures provide that funds generated by the LIR program may be expended only upon receipt by the University Accounting Office of a voucher approved by the Director and, in some cases, by the Dean of Continuing Education.

PURCHASING OF GOODS AND SERVICES

As LIR is a program of the University, all purchases of goods or services for the program must follow University procedures, as is the case for all other Continuing Education programs. This means that the Director must approve in advance all purchases for the LIR program. When the LIR Council wishes to obtain certain goods or services, it may not contract for them directly. However, the Council may recommend to the University staff assigned to the program that certain goods and services be purchased.

PROGRAM CHARGES FOR STAFF SUPPORT

Continuing Education, like many units of the University, is a cost-recovery unit and accordingly must charge for its facilities, equipment, and services. As a program of Continuing Education, the LIR program will be charged according to the schedule of campus rates, the least expensive of University rates. Information on these charges is available from the Continuing Education Office of the University.

ADMINISTRATION OF THE PROGRAM

The foregoing description of administrative procedures as they apply to the LIR program suggests the following sharing of functions:

The LIR Council determines curriculum; plans social activities; secures and confirms lecturers and instructors; writes thank-you letters to lecturers and instructors; makes appearances before groups and media on behalf of the program; assists with registration, inquiries about the program, and preparation of mailings; and provides other counsel and assistance.

The Director has administrative responsibility and is assisted by the paid staff. The paid staff is responsible for program development, advertising, registration, accounting, communications on business matters, room and equipment arrangements, and mailings. In some of these functions, volunteers from the LIR membership can be of valuable assistance.

CHAIN OF APPROVAL

As with any large organization, the University has its chain of approval. A typical routing for administrative approval of matters relating to programs begins with a member of the paid staff, whose request is forwarded to the Director for approval; then, depending upon the nature of the item, it may be forwarded to the Dean of Continuing Education and sometimes to more senior levels.

If a request or question is first taken to a dean, vice president, or more senior officer, the matter will be sent in reverse order to the initiating point, for first-stage approval or explanation. Because of this "chain of approval," it will be most efficient for questions or requests having to do with the LIR program to be taken first to the paid staff member assigned to the program or to the Director of Continuing Education.

VII

Additional Resources

The following information relating to individuals, associations, and resource materials may be of value to those involved with LIR programs.

Elderhostel Institute Network
Dr. James Verschueren
University of New Hampshire
15 Garrison Avenue
Durham, NH 03820
603-862-2055

National University Continuing Education Association
Division of Continuing Education for Older Adults
One DuPont Circle, Suite 615
Washington, DC 20036-1168
202-659-3130

"New Programs for a New Population"
(Videotape)
University of Delaware
FOCUS Program
Division of Continuing Education
John M. Clayton Hall
Newark, DE 19716
1-800-833-6287

Handbook for Learning in Retirement Organizations and Institutes
by Francis A. Meyers
Association of Learning in Retirement Organizations, West (ALIROW)
c/o The Plato Society
University of California—Los Angeles
UCLA Extension
1083 Gayley Avenue
Los Angeles, CA 90024
213-825-7917

Bibliography

ATCHLEY, R. C.. *Aging: Continuity and Change*. Belmont, CA: Wadsworth Publishing Co., 1983.

BOYLE, PATRICK G.. "Mission Statement", National Association of State Universities and Land-Grant Colleges, Washington, D.C., January 1991.

BROOKFIELD, STEPHEN D.. *Understanding and Facilitating Adult Learning*. San Francisco: Jossey–Bass, 1986.

Bureau of the Census. *Population Profile of the United States*, Current Population Report, Special Studies, U.S. Department of Commerce, Washington, D.C., No. 145, pp. 7–35, 1985.

BUTLER, ROBERT N.. "The Life Review: An Interpretation of Reminiscence in the Aged." *Psychiatry,* Vol. 26, pp. 65–76, Feb. 26, 1963.

CHICKERING, ARTHUR D.. *Education and Identity*. San Francisco: Jossey–Bass, 1969.

———. *The Modern American College: Responding to the New Realities of Diverse Students and a Changing Society*. San Francisco: Jossey–Bass, 1981.

COLE, THOMAS R.. "The 'Enlightened' View of Aging: Victorian Morality in a New Key," in Thomas R. Cole and Sally A. Gadow (eds.), *What Does It Mean to Grow Old?* Durham: Duke University Press, 1986.

CORBIN, DAVID E., JOSIE METAL-CORBIN, and DONA M. KAGAN. "Content Analysis of an Intergenerational Unit on Aging in a Sixth-Grade Classroom." *Educational Gerontology,* 1987, Vol. 13, No. 5, pp. 403–410.

COURTENAY, BRADLEY C.. "Education for Older Adults," in *Handbook of Adult and Continuing Education*. San Francisco: Jossey–Bass, 1989.

Bureau of the Census. *Current Population Reports*, Series P-25, No. 1044, 1989.

DERENZO, E. G.. "Older Learners: The Lessons They Teach Us Apply to All Students." *Aging Network News,* April 1990.

DOBROF, ROSE. "Introduction: A Time for Reclaiming the Past," in Marc Kaminsky (ed.), *The Uses of Reminiscence: New Ways of Working with Older Adults*. New York: The Haworth Press, 1984.

DYCHTWALD, KEN, and JOE FLOWER. *Age Wave*. Los Angeles: Jeremy P. Tarcher, Inc., 1989.

ERIKSON, ERIC. *Childhood and Society*. New York: Norton Press, 1963.

FIRMAN, JAMES, DONALD E. GELFAND, and CATHERINE VENTURA. "Intergenerational Service-Learning: Contributions to Curricula." *Educational Gerontology*, 1983, Vol. 9, Nos. 5–6, pp. 405–415.

HAVIGHURST, ROBERT J.. *Developmental Tasks and Education (3d ed.)*. New York: McKay, 1972.

JACOB, PHILIP E.. *Changing Values in College*. New York: Harper, 1957.

KAMINSKY, MARC. "Transfiguring Life: Images of Continuity Hidden Among the Fragments," in M. Kaminsky (ed.), *The Uses of Reminiscence* [see Dobrof, above].

KATZ, J.. "Personality and Interpersonal Relations in the College Classroom," in Nevitt Sanford (ed.), *The American College*, pp. 365–395. New York: Wiley, 1962.

KELLER, J. M.. "The Sharing of Life and Learning—An Intergenerational Program." *Lifelong Learning*, March 1983, pp. 26–27.

KNOTT, E. S.. "A Philosophical Consideration of the Relevance of Paulo Freire for the Education of Older Adults," in *Lifelong Learning Research Conference Proceedings*. MD: College Park, Department of Agriculture and Extension Education, 1983.

KNOWLES, MALCOLM S.. *The Adult Learner: A Neglected Species*. Houston: Gulf Publishing, 1973.

KNOX, ALAN B.. *Adult Development and Learning*. San Francisco: Jossey–Bass, 1977.

LANGER, ELLEN. *Mindfulness*, p. 195. Reading, MA: Addison–Wesley, 1989.

LASLETT, PETER. *A Fresh Map of Life: The Emergence of the Third Age*. London: Weidenfeld & Nicolson, 1989.

LEVINSON, DAVID J.: *The Seasons of a Man's Life:* New York: Knopf, 1978.

LONG, HUEY B.. *Adult and Continuing Education*. New York: Teachers College Press, 1983.

LONGINO, CHARLES F., JR.. "The Comfortably Retired and the Pension Elite." *American Demographics*, June 1988, pp. 22–25.

MANHEIMER, RONALD J.. "The Narrative Quest in Qualitative Gerontology." *Journal of Aging Studies*, Vol. 3, No. 3, 1989.

———. "The Politics and Promise of Cultural Enrichment Programs." *Generations*, Winter 1987–88.

MAYS, R.. "Learning in Retirement," speech given before the Torch Club of Durham and Chapel Hill, NC, September 20, 1989, pp. 2–3.

MASLOW, ABRAHAM H.. *Motivation and Personality (2d ed.)*. New York: Harper & Row, 1970.

MEYERS, F. A.. *The Handbook for Learning in Retirement Organizations and Institutes*. Los Angeles: The Association of Learning in Retirement Organizations—Western Region, 1989.

MOODY, HARRY R.. *Abundance of Life, Human Development Policies for an Aging Society.* New York: Columbia University Press, 1988.

———. "Philosophical Presuppositions of Education for Old Age." *Educational Gerontology,* Vol. 1.

MOYER, IVAN, JR., and DAN LAGO. "Institutional Barriers to Older Learners in Higher Education: A Critique of Fee-Waiver Programs." *Educational Gerontology,* 1987, Vol. 13, No. 2, 157–169.

OSTROFF, JEFF. "An Aging Market." *American Demographics,* May 1989, p. 26–37.

PEACOCK, E. WINNIFRED, and WILLIAM M. TALLEY. "Intergenerational Contact: A Way to Counteract Ageism." *Educational Gerontology,* 1984, Vol. 10, Nos. 1–2, 13–24.

PERRY, WILLIAM G., JR.. *Forms of Intellectual and Ethical Development in the College Years.* New York: Holt, Reinhart & Winston, 1970.

PETERSON, DAVID A.. "Aging and Higher Education," in J. Thornton and J. Birnen (eds.), *Education and Aging.* Englewood Cliffs: Prentice–Hall, 1987.

———. *Facilitating Education for Older Learners.* San Francisco: Jossey–Bass, 1983.

QUEENEY, DONNA S. (ED.). *An Agenda for Action: Continuing Professional Education Focus Group Reports.* University Park, PA: Pennsylvania State University, 1990.

RUSK, JEREMY. *Harvard Magazine,* May–June 1985, p. 56G.

SAMPSON, ANTHONY, and SALLY SAMPSON. *The Oxford Book of Ages.* New York: Oxford University Press, 1988.

SPARLING, JOYCE W., and JOAN C. ROGERS. "Intergenerational Intervention: A Reciprocal Service Delivery System for Preschoolers, Adolescents, and Older Persons." *Educational Gerontology,* 1985, Vol. 11, No. 1, pp. 41–55.

SPROUSE, BETSY M.. "Educational Format Preferences of Older Learners." *The Gerontologist,* 1982, Vol. 22, p. 71.

STERN, MILTON R.. "A Generation in Command: Higher Education's Role in Retirement Learning." Occasional paper. Washington, DC: National University Continuing Education Association, 1989.

WEATHERSBY, RITA. "A Developmental Perspective on Adults' Uses of Formal Education." Unpublished doctoral dissertation, Harvard University, 1977.

———. "Life Stages and Learning Interests." Paper presented at National Conference on Higher Education, N.p., 1978.

WIGDOR, BLOSSOM. "Lifelong Learning: Capturing Human Potential at All Ages." *Expression* (Newsletter of the Canadian National Advisory Council on Aging), Vol. 5, Nos. 3–4, 1989.

WILLING, J. Z.. *The Reality of Retirement,* p. 76. New York: William Morrow & Co., 1981.

WINTER, A., and R. WINTER. *Build Your Brain Power: The Latest Techniques to Preserve, Restore and Improve Your Brain's Potential.* New York: St. Martin's Press, 1986.

Index

A

Academic standards, 61–65
Academies, 18
Admission, 79
Adult development, 116–117
Age-integrated, 114–115, 128–129
Age-segregated, 113, 114, 116, 121
Age Wave, 15
Ages of man, 16
Aging
  American population, 2
  better educated, 15
  comfortably retired, 15
  demographics, 2, 14
  estimated U.S. population change, 14*t*.
American University, 26
  Institute for Learning in Retirement, 30, 32, 35, 57
Andragogy, 113–114
Art courses, 65
Asnuntuck Community College
  University of the Third Age, 31
Atchley, Robert, 108

B

Benefits
  higher education, 21
  intellectual, 103–106
  member, 69–72, 81
  social, 104–106
Blazey, Mark L., *xi*
Brooklyn College
  Institute for Retired Professionals and Executives, 26, 34, 55, 66, 107
Broomall, James K., *xi*
Budget. *See also* Fees
  financial aid, 96
  first year, 160–161
  fiscal control, 85
  grants, 86–87
  models, 88–89, 160–161
  standard costs, 95–96
  start-up costs, 86
  treasurer, 86, 94–95
Butler, Robert N., 124
Buxbaum, Edwin, 110

C

California State University
  Renaissance Society, 55
California State University-Fullerton
  Continuing Learning Experience Institute, 58, 107, 110

171

Centenary College
   Senior Adult Education Program, 31
Central Washington University, 20
Changing attitudes, 124
Changing workforce, 15–16
Chickering, Arthur D., 116
Cobin, David E., 117
Cole, Thomas R., 131
College for Elders, 4, 5
Collins, Donald E., xi
Courtenay, Bradley C., 17, 115
Craven, Sara, xii
Creative retirement, 122–131
Cultural activities, 34
Curriculum
   committee, 32, 55
   development of, 53, 55–56
   instructional design, 53–66

D

DeRenzo, E. G., 20
Development, financial, 97
Distance learning strategies, 20
Dobrof, Rose, 124
Dues. *See* Fees
Duke University, 73, 75, 80, 86, 87, 97, 100, 110
Dychtwald, Kenneth, 15–16

E

Eckerd College
   Academy of Senior Professionals, 30–31, 65–66, 88–89, 118
Edna McConnell Clark Foundation, 86
Eesley, Jane S., xii
Elderhood, 1–3
Elderhostel, 3, 19, 55, 108, 125, 165
Enrichment programs, 65
Erikson, Eric, 116
Evaluation, 48, 61, 62
   course, 48
Experiential learning, 104

F

Facilities. *See* Space
Faculty, 59–61

outside experts, 61
payment, 61
selection, 59
skills bank, 59
Fairleigh Dickinson University—Florham-Madison Campus
   Education Program for Older Adults, 118
Fees, 33, 35, 87
   annual versus term, 90–91
   comprehensive versus per course, 33
   membership dues, 43–44, 89–91
   refunds, 92
   tuition versus fees, 90
Financing, 36. *See also* Budget, Fees
Firman, James, 117
Fischer, Richard B., xii
Five College Learning in Retirement Institute, 57, 103
Fordham University
   College at 60, 26
Founding members. *See* Marketing
Fund for the Improvement of Postsecondary Education, 118
Fund raising, 107

G

Gerontology, 130
Governance
   bylaws, 48, 143–147, 162–164
   historical records, 49
   organizational structure, 48*t*.
Grant MacEwan Community College
   Senior Studies Institute, 19
Groverton University, 4–5

H

Harvard University
   Institute for Learning in Retirement, 56, 86–89, 95, 97, 107–109
Havighurst, Robert J., 116

I

Institute model, 18
Institute network. *See* Elderhostel, 19

Instructional formats, 57–59
　meeting times, 58
Intergenerational, 113–121
　institutional applications, 117–119

J

Jacob, Phillip E., 117
Johns Hopkins University
　Evergreen Society, 55

K

KAT Program, 21
Katz, J., 117
Kingsborough Community College
　My Turn Program, 19, 26, 33, 118–119
Knowles, Malcolm S., 114
Knox, Alan B., 116
Kriedler, George, 122

L

Langer, Ellen, 109
Learning in retirement
　developing successful programs, 25–66
　educational movement, 3
　questions, 9
　reciprocities, 4
Leisure, 3, 17
Les Universites du Troisieme Age, 16
Levinson, David J., 116
Lifelong Learning Act, 125
Lipman, Henry T., *xii*
LIR Programs
　common characteristics, 28
　curriculum, 31–32
　evaluation, 33
　faculty, 32
　fees, 31
　institution-driven, 25–27
　member-driven, 26–27, 29
　membership, 30
　organization, 29
　organizational models, 25–37
　paid staff, 29

Long, Hugh B., 115, 119
Lunchroom, 80, 105

M

Manatee Junior College
　Retired Executives and Professionals, 34
Manheimer, Ronald J., *xii*
Marketing, 40, 67–83
　attracting members, 72–77
　community support, 41
　converting inquiries, 46
　course descriptions, 73–74
　distribution, 78
　founding members, 47
　initial publicity, 46
　internal, 72
　media, 75
　open house, 73
　printed materials, 73–74
　retirement communities, 75
　word of mouth, 42, 73
Maslow, Abraham H., 101
Mays, Rolland, 69
Member-driven, 1, 18
Members' views, 99–110, 134–138
　psycho-social needs, 100–103, 106–107
Membership. *See also* Marketing
　form, 148–149
　membership committees, 79–80
　name tags, 80
　turnover, 82
　types, 79
Meyers, Francis A., 166
Miller, Paul A., 1
Moody, Harry, 124
Moyer, Harry R., 117
Mumford, Lewis, 138

N

National Council on the Aging
　Senior Center Humanities Program, 125
National Endowment for the Arts, 125

National Endowment for the Humanities, 125
National University Continuing Education Association, 18–19, 30, 165
  survey, 150–152
New School for Social Research
  Institute for Retired Professionals, 26, 34, 56, 58, 65, 93, 103, 105, 114, 125
Nisbet, Robert, 6
Northwestern University, 87, 93, 97, 105

O

Oasis Centers, 3
Ortega y Gasset, 5
Outreach, 65, 76

P

Paid staff, 51, 88, 92–93
Parking, 77
Peacock, E. Winnifred, 115, 117
Peer teaching, 45–46, 56
Perry, William G., 116–117
Peterson, David A., 19, 114–115, 116
Pima County Community College
  Senior Education Program, 88–89, 93
Political support, 44
Post-retirement learners
  college and university responsibilities, 17
Post-retirement learning, 13–21
Prairies Visionaries, 20
Privileges, 54, 64

Q

Queeney, Donna S., 16

R

Recruitment. See Marketing
Retention. See Marketing
Retirement rite, 6–8
Retreats, 81–82
Rochester Institute of Technology, 76

Rusk, Jeremy, 95, 97, 109
Ryerson Polytechnical Institute
  Program in Intergenerational Learning, 119

S

San Diego State University-Rancho Bernardo, 57
San Diego State University-San Diego, 57
Scheduling, 76–77
Scholarship, 107
Senior colleges, 18
Senior Ventures, 20
Size, 34–35, 58
  class limits, 34
Social activities, 33–34, 43, 77
Southern Illinois University-Edwardsville
  Metro-East Institute for Lifetime Learning, 30
Southern Oregon State College, 20
Space, 42–43, 51, 57, 76–77, 96
Sparling, Joyce W., 117
Sponsoring institutions, 153–159*t*.
Springfield College, 104
Sprouse, Betsy M., 115
Starting a program, 38–52
Stern, Milton, *xii*
Student status, 33

T

Temple University
  Center for Intergenerational Learning, 120
  Temple Association for Retired Professionals, 30, 33–34, 109
Term length, 76
Third age, 8, 16
Travel, 54
Tuition. See Fees
Tuition waiver, 19

U

University commitment, 39–40

University of California-Berkeley
  Center for Learning in Retirement, 33, 35, 100, 105
University of California-Los Angeles
  Plato Society, 30–31, 56, 57, 64, 72, 86, 93, 114, 118
University of California-San Diego
  Institute for Continued Learning, 70
University of Delaware
  Academy of Lifelong Learning, 21, 26, 33–35, 41, 73, 76, 86, 97, 100, 107, 110, 113
University of Lowell
  Learning in Retirement Association, 88
University of Massachusetts, 130
University of Miami
  Institute for Retired Professionals, 76, 100
University of North Carolina-Asheville
  Center for Creative Retirement, 19, 122, 126
  College for Seniors, 118, 122, 127
  Creative Seniors Leadership Program, 127
  Senior Academy for Intergenerational Learning, 118, 123, 128
University of Regina
  Senior Education Center, 20

University of Wisconsin-Milwaukee, 18

V

Videotape, 165
Virginia Commonwealth University, 33
  Open University, 31
Volunteers, 45, 52, 93–94
  structure, 45

W

Weathersby, Rita, 116
Weber State College, 20
Western Washington University
  Bridge at Bellingham, 119
Wigdor, Blossom, 16
Willing, Jules, 69
Winter, A., 18
Winter, R., 18

Y

Young, Kenneth E., xii

Z

Zissis, Cecilia, 136